"*The Soul Online* covers very timely information related to grief and the digital age and connects current events to historical and recent societal trends. . . . The information presented is examined in a theoretical and scholarly manner and offers recommendations relevant to counseling and pastoral practitioners. I would recommend this book to those who work with grieving individuals and families."

—NADINE PELLING
Clinical Psychologist and Senior Lecturer in Clinical Psychology and Counseling, University of South Australia

"Sharing our suffering and sorrow and receiving help and care online is a relatively new dynamic and one that Geldenhuys and Hill have diligently and creatively explored. This is an extraordinarily thoughtful and timely book. . . . *The Soul Online* is indeed an essential contribution to human flourishing! I was encouraged and challenged and immensely enjoyed reading this book. I recommend it to you."

—NICHOLAS MARKS
CEO, Australian Institute of Family Counselling

"This book is a fascinating and compelling account of new responses to the age-old question 'How do we respond to human suffering?' Geldenhuys and Hill explore the emergence of technological rituals and spiritualities through the lens of Christian theology. They offer a vital, urgently needed new framework for spiritual care and counseling in the online world that leads to wholeness of life."

—PETER SHERLOCK
Vice-Chancellor, University of Divinity

"*The Soul Online* provides *phronesis*, informed theological imagination, and serious engagement with current bereavement research and practice. Emerging from various theological and social science perspectives, *The Soul Online* provides innovative modalities for care that articulate possibilities, practices, and rituals that are ethical and efficacious. Most importantly, during times of grief and pain, *The Soul Online* enables pastors and other care professionals the resources to provide hope in a digital world."

—TIM SENSING
Associate Dean, Graduate School of Theology, Abilene Christian University

"This is a remarkable and cutting-edge book on how the digital world has transformed grieving experiences. . . . I highly recommend this book as a detailed road map for anyone who wishes to navigate the explosion of new ideas and grieving practices on social media. I count it as essential reading for chaplains, pastoral carers, and counselors."

—ART WOUTERS
Dean of Counseling, Stirling Theological College

"In this unique book, Hill and Geldenhuys explore bereavement practices in an online world. . . . Those seeking to provide personal support while managing an increasingly complex range of associated issues will benefit greatly from this book. The range of tools and techniques applicable to counseling and spiritual care practices will make this book a significant and thought-provoking resource for many."

—ROB NYHUIS
Chair, Churches of Christ Council in Australia

"What a journey this book leads us on—I will be back to reread this book and ponder anew how the body of Christ is called to be with people in pain. I would recommend this book to explore the changing world, especially regarding grief work in our digital world."

—ROB SALMON
Counselor, Supervisor, and Counseling Lecturer

"I found *The Soul Online* an enthralling account and review of the current online community of mourners utilizing social networking sites to grieve. . . . It reveals new methods of mourning, including continuing bonds between the living and deceased, an expectation of an afterlife, and identities shared, persevered, and revisited regularly with online communication. This book is an exceptionally well-researched read from both a theological and practical viewpoint."

—TRACEY MILSON
Clinical Counselor, Family Therapist, and Counseling Educator

"God is with us in all our suffering. But how does this apply in online interaction and care? Hill and Geldenhuys investigate opportunities and anxieties for digital practices, including netiquette for friends and support groups, best practices for counselors and the funeral industry, the distress of dark tourism and mourning trolls, and controversial options on digital ghosts. This short book opens many areas for fruitful discussion. It will be useful for practitioners, trainers, and anyone wishing to show care and concern through technology or social media."

—JILL FIRTH
Theological College Lecturer, Anglican Priest, and Spiritual Director

The Soul Online

The Soul Online

Bereavement, Social Media,
and Competent Care

GRAHAM JOSEPH HILL
and DESIREE GELDENHUYS

CASCADE *Books* • Eugene, Oregon

THE SOUL ONLINE
Bereavement, Social Media, and Competent Care

Copyright © 2022 Graham Joseph Hill and Desiree Geldenhuys. All rights reserved. Except for brief quotations in critical publications or reviews, no part of this book may be reproduced in any manner without prior written permission from the publisher. Write: Permissions, Wipf and Stock Publishers, 199 W. 8th Ave., Suite 3, Eugene, OR 97401.

Cascade Books
An Imprint of Wipf and Stock Publishers
199 W. 8th Ave., Suite 3
Eugene, OR 97401

www.wipfandstock.com

PAPERBACK ISBN: 978-1-7252-6650-6
HARDCOVER ISBN: 978-1-7252-6651-3
EBOOK ISBN: 978-1-7252-6652-0

Cataloguing-in-Publication data:

Names: Hill, Graham Joseph, author. | Geldenhuys, Desiree, author.

Title: The soul online : bereavement, social media, and competent care / Graham Joseph Hill and Desiree Geldenhuys.

Description: Eugene, OR: Cascade Books, 2022 | Includes bibliographical references.

Identifiers: ISBN 978-1-7252-6650-6 (paperback) | ISBN 978-1-7252-6651-3 (hardcover) | ISBN 978-1-7252-6652-0 (ebook)

Subjects: LCSH: Internet—Religious aspects. | Death—Psychological aspects. | Grief. | Virtual reality—Social aspects.

Classification: BL37 S35 2022 (paperback) | BL37 (ebook)

VERSION NUMBER 122721

Contents

Introduction: Suffering, Loss, Social Media, and Competent Care | 1

1 Outlining the Emerging Phenomenon | 15
2 Comparing Traditional Caucasian Euro-American and Digital Bereavement Practices | 28
3 Bereavement, Embodiment, and Cybergnosticism: Foundational Issues | 36
4 Bereavement, Embodiment, and Cybergnosticism: Specific Issues | 53
5 Evaluating Therapeutic Responses to Bereavement Practices in the Digital Age | 76
6 Constructing New Bereavement Practices in the Digital Age | 92
7 Proposals for Bereavement Counseling and Pastoral and Spiritual Care in a Digital Age | 101
8 Recommendations for Further Research and Study | 113
9 Competent Care of the Soul Online | 119

Bibliography | 123
About the Authors | 133

Introduction
Suffering, Loss, Social Media, and Competent Care

The pandemic has led to increased suffering, death, and loss across the world. Many have lost people they love. Mourning, grief, and bereavement are widespread.

In Matthew 5:4, Jesus says, "Blessed are those who mourn, for they shall be comforted." The picture is from Isaiah 61:1–3:

> The Spirit of the Sovereign LORD is on me because the LORD has anointed me to preach good news to the poor. He has sent me to bind up the broken-hearted, to proclaim freedom for the captives and release from darkness for the prisoners, to proclaim the year of the LORD's favor and the day of vengeance of our God, to comfort all who mourn, and provide for those who grieve in Zion—to bestow on them a crown of beauty instead of ashes, the oil of gladness instead of mourning, and a garment of praise instead of a spirit of despair. They will be called oaks of righteousness, a planting of the LORD for the display of his splendor.

How is it possible that God can bless those who mourn? And how are they comforted? C. S. Lewis once wrote: "We were promised sufferings. They were part of the program. We were even told, 'Blessed are they that mourn,' and I accept it. I've got nothing that I hadn't bargained for. Of course it is different when the thing happens to oneself, not to others, and in reality, not imagination."[1]

Many people's lives are full of suffering. How do we make sense of this suffering? Why does God allow suffering? Why does God allow the innocent and righteous to suffer? Where is God when I'm hurting and mourning?

An older adult groans in pain, longing for release. A young woman loses her husband in a motorbike accident, leaving her to raise her three children alone. We cringe at the horror of Auschwitz. We see the millions of people this year who have lost their health, lives, or loved ones to the COVID-19 pandemic.

We're confronted and offended by such misery. We often search for hidden meaning contained within suffering itself, or we seek explanations from other places.

WHAT DOES THE BIBLE SAY ABOUT LOSS AND SUFFERING?

The breadth of suffering in the world raises profound questions about God's nature and involvement in human life. If God is all good, all-powerful, and all-loving, then why do the innocent suffer?

Neither the Old Testament nor the New Testament provides complete answers to this question. But some answers are given, and these ideas can be explored.

The Bible teaches that we suffer primarily because of the fallen, broken, wounded, sinful nature of humanity.[2] Sin has entered the world and brought death, disease, division, and destruction. Human beings rebel against God and God's holiness, righteousness, and justice. And human bodies and the creation are frail. But, despite this struggle, we are assured that God remains King. We

---

1. Lewis, *Grief Observed*, 32.
2. Genesis 3.

Introduction

are assured that when Christ returns, all things will be eternally restored—and this includes the end of all suffering and evil.[3]

In this life, we experience suffering and pain. These insult our sense of the world's fairness. They raise questions "about the goodness, the compassion, even the existence of God."[4]

Our friend Steve Frost recently taught from Jesus' parable of the Mustard Seed.[5] We often misunderstand the parable. In a world addicted to the shiny, successful, eye-catching, and exponentially growing, the kingdom of God is almost embarrassingly ordinary. But it's perfect for rest, shade, and food. The sun continues to beat down on people, scorching them and causing them to suffer.

The kingdom of God is rest and shade and renewal and hope, but it isn't some giant umbrella that protects us from all pain. But there's hope! Even as the sun beats down, in that very same moment, the kingdom of God provides rest and shade and food. It provides healing and hope and new life amid pain and suffering. That's the good news.

WHAT DOES JOB SAY ABOUT LOSS AND SUFFERING?

The Old Testament book of Job is one source that Christians and Jews turn to explain human suffering and pain. Job is a stunning ancient text. It helps us engage with both the conceptual problems of suffering and the human, interpersonal, gut-level experiences. The misery of innocent, defenseless, and good people is a dilemma.

Job is a righteous man who lives a blameless and upright life, fearing God and shunning evil. Despite this, he suffers greatly. He loses livestock, friends, property, health, and his sons and daughters. One calamity is added to the next.

---

3. Colossians 2:15; cf. 1 Corinthians 15:54–57; Revelation 12:10–12.

4. Kushner, "Why Do the Righteous Suffer?," 316. See Kushner, *When Bad Things Happen*.

5. Matthew 13:31–32. Steve Frost gave this talk at the Baptist Churches of NSW/ACT Revive Conference at Dural Baptist Church, Sydney, in May 2017.

In the story, Job's three friends come to "comfort" him in his suffering and loss. But their "comfort" is nothing like God's comfort. Job's friends believed in a doctrine of divine retribution—a belief that God rewards the righteous and punishes the wicked in this life. But Job questioned this theology when his experience seemed in blatant contradiction to its proposals and convictions.

Why do some people embrace the doctrine of divine retribution to explain pain and suffering?

- To understand, control, and protect God's image as both omnipotent and good.
- To preserve religious and theological traditions.
- To use an ethical or moral motivation.

But what are some of the results?

- The condemnation of fellow human beings.
- The sufferer is forced to blame themself.
- God is relegated to the position of adversary.
- No satisfactory answer is provided for the sufferer.

WHEN THE RIGHTEOUS AND INNOCENT SUFFER AND MOURN

The book of Job denies the doctrine of divine retribution. Job's friends hold rigidly to the principle of divine punishment and encourage Job to repent. They say that if he repents, he'll escape his suffering and receive God's blessing. In doing so, they "unsuspectingly tempt him to use God for his personal gain, [which is] the essence of sin."[6] If Job had followed their counsel, he would have vindicated his accusers who claimed that human beings seek personal gain in their worship of God. Using the words of the three

---

6. Hartley, *Job*, 48.

Introduction

"comforters," the author of Job "strongly denounces the practice of using deceptive arguments to defend God."[7]

The book of Job offers no definitive answer to the problem of human misery. The issue is ventilated, and Job's friends offer partial answers. But, in the end, "readers cannot discover from the book any one clear view about what the reason for their own particular suffering may be, nor any statement about the reason for human suffering in general; for the book is entirely about the suffering of one particular and unique individual."[8]

The book of Job doesn't deny that sufferers deserve suffering sometimes. Yet, it contradicts the idea that this is always the case. Job exemplifies the innocent sufferer, whose innocence is asserted by the story's narrator, the holy God, and Job himself.

The book of Job tells us that the righteous and innocent may suffer terribly and that adverse circumstances do not necessarily witness to an individual's moral corruption. Righteous and innocent people may suffer deeply in every sphere of life (physical, social, spiritual, and emotional).

FORGET CLEVER ANSWERS TO THE MEANING OF SUFFERING

Job doesn't portray the suffering of the righteous, innocent, and good as something that's necessarily cleansing, educational, testing, or edifying. The author upholds the goodness of both God and Job. But human will, the laws of nature, human sin, and the brokenness of the world all combine to contribute to the suffering of the innocent, exculpating God and the sufferer from responsibility.

Yet even these "clever" explanations don't heal the wounds or satisfy the objections of the millions who suffer. There is no clear answer to the question of human suffering in the book of Job.

---

7. Hartley, *Job*, 49.
8. Clines, *Job 1–20*, xxxviii.

The mistake of Job's friends was that they offered complicated explanations to an innocent sufferer who needed comfort, support, and sympathy. He didn't need their clichéd or "clever" answers.

We learn from Job that God is not predictable, and it is entirely acceptable to question God when we are in pain. But no thorough explanation to human misery is provided nor attempted in the book.

The problem of suffering (as distinct from the experience of suffering) is a monotheist problem only. Only the monotheist asks, "How can the one true God be omnipotent, good, and compassionate when the innocent and righteous suffer?" A polytheistic, pantheistic, or atheistic view of the world doesn't need to ask such a question. For the monotheist, misery has a moral or ethical quality attached to it. It is seen as bad, wrong, and unjust, and it needs to be reconciled with our understanding of the one good God.

But the book of Job, to the frustration of many monotheists, is not a theodicy. A theodicy is an attempt to justify God's ways to human beings (or an attempt to vindicate divine providence in the face of evil and suffering). Theodicies strive to resolve the problem of evil and suffering for a theological system. They seek to demonstrate that God is omnipotent, all-loving, and just—despite the existence of misery and evil.

Job, however, is primarily the personal account of one man's unique experiences of suffering.

The book is about his wrestle with the meaning of human misery. It's far removed from the Augustinian theodicy (evil is a perversion of goodness arising from humanity's abuse of free will), the Irenaean theodicy (free will and evil are soul-building), or the Leibnizian theodicy (the existing world is the best of all possible worlds that God could have created). It's not a theodicy because Job doesn't attempt to explain the problem of suffering and evil.

At the same time, Job rejects the doctrine of corruption (everyone suffers because everything is corrupt). And it rejects the stoic idea that we are required to transcend our misfortunes in this life and receive our reward in the next.

Introduction

Terrence W. Tilley was correct when he wrote that the book of Job "displays the cost of providing the 'systematic totalization' a theodicy requires: silencing the voice of the sufferer, even if s/he curses the day s/he was born and accuses God of causing human suffering."[9]

In the book of Job, theodicies are at best represented as the impetuous young Elihu, who is full of hot air. Or, at worst, they are "not quite torturers, but all the forms of intimidation, all the psychological conditionings, are good for them to obtain the famous spontaneous confessions so dear to dictatorial societies."[10] The book of Job develops no coherent theodicy. It provides no theological foundations for establishing a modern theodicy. That is not the purpose of this ancient drama.

IT'S OK TO QUESTION GOD

In the book, Job is never condemned for questioning God. In desperate anguish, he gropes for answers in the dark abyss of his misery. He laments his bitter feelings and grievous calamities. He cries to God for a response.

Job questions God vigorously—not logically or consistently, but as one motivated by grief and inner turmoil. "Job legitimates our feelings toward God and religion when we suffer intensely for no discernible reason."[11]

Job is convinced that he's become a mockery to his neighbor. He knows that, although he is blameless, he is a laughingstock to those around him. Job says, "I want to speak with the Almighty; I wish to reason with God."[12] God then allows Job to question God unashamedly, forthrightly, and openly.

God is more offended by inauthentic piety or dogmatic orthodoxy than by those who love God and who ask God direct

---

9. Tilley, "Silencing of Job," 267.
10. Tilley, "Silencing of Job," 267.
11. Di Lella, "Existential Interpretation," 51.
12. Job 13:3.

questions—including questions about the meaning of their misery. God doesn't require that we repress our anger or grief. God doesn't need us to settle for petty or trite answers about the nature, meaning, and origins of evil and suffering.

The book of Job legitimates "the quest of believers for self-understanding and meaning, while at the same time encouraging them to display emotional integrity and candor in their relationships with God and others."[13]

Once Job has aired his criticisms and questions of God, he encounters God's majesty and is overwhelmed that God would even reason with him. In his encounter with God, he finds profound personal meaning amid undeserved suffering. God responded to Job's cries of anguish in this encounter. This is because the author of the book of Job believes that God responds to human misery—sometimes incomprehensibly, often unfathomably, but always with compassion.

When Jesus says, "Blessed are those who mourn, for they will be comforted" (or "for God is their comforter"), he is picking up on a deeply held conviction among God's people, over countless generations.

God responds to Job's questioning. But God doesn't do it in a manner that would silence through fear, placate with logical explanations, or bribe to keep Job silent. Instead, God responds by being present with Job in a relationship and allows Job to meet God through his compassion, healing, love, and even sorrow.

The book of Job tells us that human beings have the responsibility to pursue and display morality, compassion, justice, freedom, and hope in the face of suffering and injustice. That's a central theme in the Beatitudes and the Sermon on the Mount too.

The book of Job is scathing of Job's friends (just as Jesus was of the religious leaders) and their easy, clever, and clichéd answers to the problem of evil and suffering. Job shows us that when people suffer, we should listen to them compassionately instead of offering them clichéd answers that do not satisfy their pain. We also learn that we should trust in the goodness of God to work everything

---

13. Di Lella, "Existential Interpretation," 55.

out in the end and to fill us with God's surprising and inexplicable comfort.

The book's message is that there is no rigid answer to these difficult questions, and that it's acceptable to question God. We don't have to settle for superficial answers to the problem of suffering and evil. Life is full of contradictions and pain. The righteous and innocent sufferer may find hope and peace in trusting God, even if they can't find satisfactory answers to their painful questions.

SO, WHERE IS GOD WHEN IT HURTS AND WHEN WE MOURN?

The question remains, if God takes pleasure in us, then why do the innocent suffer illness, violence, loss, and bereavement? Here are some responses. But keep in mind what we have said about the unsatisfactory nature of simplistic answers when we, or someone we love, is experiencing suffering.

1. God Suffers

The Bible shows us a God who does not distance Godself from human suffering. God suffers. And God suffers greatly. Jesus experienced profound suffering: physical (from hunger, weariness, flogging, crucifixion), emotional (he wept for Lazarus and grieved for the fall of his people), and mental and spiritual (such as his agony in the garden and torment on the cross).

Jesus identifies with innocent sufferers because he was an innocent sufferer. When Jesus said, "Blessed are those who mourn, for they will be comforted," he knew that from experience. And he likely anticipated his suffering on the cross.

Paul describes Christ as our intercessor in heaven who profoundly understands, shares, and experiences our sufferings—because he has suffered. God is a suffering God. God is the "crucified God." God won't know the end of God's pain and heartbreak over our suffering until the restoration of all things through Christ (i.e., the second coming). We are not alone in our pain, for when we suffer, God suffers with us.

2. God is Present, Even in Our Suffering

Since God is involved in our suffering, God can work through it for our good (even though suffering is never good in itself). Since God's presence is with us when we suffer, God may use suffering to draw us to Christ, develop in us Christian maturity, and accomplish God's purposes. (Note that we've said God *uses* not *causes* suffering for God's people. It's still an unsettling thought, though—God *uses* pain to bring us to God.)[14]

As C. S. Lewis once famously wrote, "God whispers to us in our pleasures, speaks in our conscience, but shouts in our pain: it is His megaphone to rouse a deaf world."[15] Lewis says that suffering can lead us to humility and dependency on God. (But suffering can also lead us to final and unrepentant rebellion.) Suffering can also break down our wrong ideas about God. Suffering can (but doesn't always) lead to hope. And suffering only makes sense in the light of the final chapter—the new heaven and new earth in Jesus Christ.

3. God Gives Us Hope and Comfort

The New Testament brings an entirely new perspective to our understanding of suffering: the perspective of eternity. Paul wrote to a people whom Rome tortured, persecuted, and tormented, and society often marginalized and despised. These Christians often experienced grief, loss, and bereavement. "The sufferings of this present time are not worthy to be compared with the glory that will be revealed in us."[16]

---

14. See Hebrews 5:8; 1 Peter 1:7.
15. Lewis, *Problem of Pain*, 91.
16. Romans 8:18.

Introduction

We suffer in this life. Faith doesn't protect us from that. Indeed, we're promised suffering if we follow Christ.

But the Bible says that we can hope in the new heaven and the new earth, where there will be no more pain or suffering. This life is as a drop in the ocean compared with our eternal peace, joy, and wholeness with God. Such thoughts don't always comfort us when we suffer or lose someone we love. But, at times, such hope helps to make the suffering of this life more bearable—and directs our hearts and minds to our eternal hope in Jesus Christ.

The meaning of human misery will perplex us for as long as suffering exists. Why does suffering exist? What is its origin or cause? Why am I personally suffering? Why do the righteous and innocent suffer if God is just, all-powerful, and all-loving? What is the meaning of human misery?

The message of the book of Job is that there's no rigid answer to these difficult questions. And it's acceptable to question God. We don't have to settle for superficial answers to the problem of suffering and evil. Life is full of ambiguities, paradoxes, and uncertainties. Yet, somehow, amid this chaos, God works out God's purposes—offering hope, healing, peace, new life, and comfort for those who mourn.

Our God is a "crucified God." Our God is a "suffering God." Our God is present with us in our suffering. Our God has suffered and continues to suffer.

But our God is also the "resurrected and returning God," who offers the hope of the new creation and the restoration of all things. God's glory will be revealed in us. Our God is the God who comforts those who mourn.

Suffering and loss are made bearable in the light of God's presence, God's comfort, and God's final plan—the restoration of all things, at the end of the age, in Jesus Christ. You and I will suffer in this life. But the Bible says to those who mourn: "the sufferings of this present time are not worthy to be compared with the glory that will be revealed in us."[17]

---

17. Romans 8:18.

And Jesus says to us, "Blessed are the poor and humble, who realize their sin and spiritual emptiness and poverty, for theirs is the kingdom of heaven. Blessed also are those who mourn, for they will be comforted."[18]

SUFFERING, LOSS, AND BEREAVEMENT IN THE DIGITAL AGE

How people process their suffering, loss, and bereavement has shifted in the digital age. This brings us to the primary themes of this book: bereavement, social media, and competent care.

The growing phenomenon of online interactions by the bereaved with the online presence of their deceased loved ones has recently come to the attention of caring professionals. How do we understand digital memorialization, online identities, and continuing bonds? How do we respond to digital bereavement communities and new digital death and bereavement rituals and practices? How do we think about technospirituality, cybergnosticism, and the digital afterlife?[19]

In this book, we examine existing therapeutic responses to death and bereavement practices and evaluate the efficacy in meeting mourners' needs in a digital context. We explore the rising interest in spirituality and the phenomenon of technospirituality, including interest in the afterlife. We outline new death and bereavement practices in the digital public sphere as mourners address their own bereavement needs intentionally and inadvertently. We help therapeutic and death practitioners construct considered practices to meet these needs. Finally, we develop new counseling, pastoral, and spiritual care proposals to address the needs of the bereaved.

The digital age has enabled people to interact online individually and in online communities for loss, grief, memorialization, identity formation, death and bereavement rituals, digital

---

18. Matthew 5:3–4.

19. One of the first uses of the term "technospirituality" was by Bell. See Bell, "No More SMS."

Introduction

immortality, and spirituality. Facebook has become an unstoppable digital graveyard where ordinary people can leave legacies and provide opportunities for the bereaved to interact with "them" beyond death. The "digital souls" of the bereaved live on to enhance their bereaved loved ones' lives. Alternatively, their "digital presence" serves as a "digital ghost" to prolong loss and pain, impacting our traditional mourning and grieving processes and practices.

We outline some of what we know about this context and phenomena. This study enables us to reflect on the implications for counseling, pastoral, and spiritual carers. We also evaluate existing therapeutic responses to loss and grief and death practices.

Chapter 1 outlines the emerging phenomena, exploring how people in modern societies are changing the way they think about death, dying, and grief. Digital legacies, digital wills, digital afterlife, digital souls, digital identities, digital immortality, and digital communities are increasing. Chapter 2 compares traditional Caucasian Euro-American and digital bereavement practices. We investigate the interplay between rituals, spirituality, religion, and technology. Chapter 3 considers whether what we are seeing is a form of "cybergnosticism." We examine Gnosticism of the second and third centuries and its key features and ideologies. The only way to know if grief-related technospirituality and digital memorialization are cybergnostic is to understand Gnosticism and to see if the emerging phenomena fit. Chapter 4 takes that analysis further. This chapter focuses on the specific perspectives of Gnosticism, online bereavement, and digital memorialization. These perspectives relate to human personhood, community, and engagement with the world and social behavior. Chapter 5 evaluates therapeutic responses to bereavement practices in the digital age. Chapter 6 looks at how people construct new bereavement practices in the digital age. Chapter 7 offers proposals for bereavement counseling and pastoral and spiritual care in the digital age. Recognizing this is a largely unexamined field, chapter 8 makes proposals for further research and study. Finally, chapter 9 is an appeal for competent care online.

Several questions emerge: Why does a bereaved individual continue to engage with the online presence of a deceased loved one regularly, over a prolonged period? What do they find there? What are they looking for "there" that traditional practices around loss and grief, ritual and memorialization do not fulfill? Could this phenomenon be indicative of changing trends in memorialization and meaning-making? Does it contribute to ongoing identity formation through rituals around death, mourning, and grieving? What are the impacts of these practices in a digital context on mourners? How does this affect or inform their spiritual practices and held beliefs?

Such an exploration compels us to explore spirituality, religion, and technospirituality and its associated "afterlife" in the context of bereavement and social media. It is time carers explored these themes and discerned implications for grief, loss, and bereavement counseling and pastoral and spiritual care.

We hope that this book helps equip counselors, pastors, and spiritual carers as they offer competent bereavement care in the digital age.

I

Outlining the Emerging Phenomenon

The digital age has generated new possibilities and emerging avenues for bereavement. We can see this in new rituals and practices to do with death and mourning, memorialization, and continuing bonds. We also observe how technologies enable continued formation and maintenance of the deceased's identity, establishing grief/bereavement communities, therapeutic approaches to grief and bereavement counseling and therapy, and more. Social Networking Sites (SNSs) such as Facebook have seen the nascent and expanding phenomenon of memorialized pages, and online interactions by the bereaved and their deceased loved one's virtual presence.

The advent of the digital age has brought irreversible and burgeoning changes to the field of thanatology or the "scientific study of death and its practices" and specifically to *thanatechnology*. Thanatechnology includes all types of technological communication used to access information and research about death and thanatology. We find thanatechnology in the fields of education, counseling, pastoral ministry, and spiritual care.[1] Tony Walter also

---

1. Sofka et al., "Thanatechnology," 3.

regards thanatology as an interdisciplinary field including the social sciences, such as sociology and psychology. He concludes that a pervasive social media culture has shifted mourners' social interactions. These shifts have occurred in new directions and returned social interactions to something resembling "pre-industrial village relationships." Such relationships reflect an "everyday awareness of mortality, greater use of religious images and potential conflicts for mourners."[2] Carla Sofka and her fellow researchers state that the expansion and advances in technology have extended how society thinks about death, dying, and grief. In our new virtual world, issues such as "digital legacies," "digital wills," "digital afterlife," "digital souls," "digital identities," "digital immortality," and "digital communities" and their effects and implications need to be considered.[3]

Social Networking Sites (SNSs) are online platforms that allow users to create public profiles and interact with other users on their platforms.[4] SNSs such as Facebook facilitate sharing messages, content, and images (photos and video clips) across groups such as family, friends, colleagues, and acquaintances for users during their lifetimes and beyond. Facebook had 2,797 million monthly active Facebook users worldwide as of the fourth quarter of 2020.[5]

Ari Stillman describes Facebook as the "default destination" for many in expressing grief and memorialization. Social media is the facilitator of delocalization of the deceased's final resting place. Facebook makes this "resting place" available to those unable to say their final goodbyes in conventional practices.[6] Facebook provides mechanisms for making funeral arrangements and announcements, notification of death and dying, attending funerals through digital connectivity, and offering online virtual memorials with increased accessibility. Online attendance of funerals and memorials

2. Walter, "New Mourners." Quoted from abstract.
3. Walter, "New Mourners." Quoted from abstract.
4. "What is a SNS?"
5. "Number of Monthly Active Facebook Users."
6. Stillman, "Virtual Graveyard," 48–49.

Outlining the Emerging Phenomenon

provides an opportunity for formulating and organizing words, reflections, and memories in private. Facebook contributes to public expressions of grief and sharing of memories—"democratizing this phenomenon by making such virtual mementos publicly accessible to experience privately."[7]

Several researchers agree that Facebook has created communities of mourners both intentionally or by default.[8] Communities of mourning are created as Facebook users, who might never have had previous contact, share and read about the deceased's memories and stories and encounter each other as co-mourners. Kathleen Gilbert and Sofka highlight the successful formation of online bereavement communities formed by adolescents, who are often regarded as more vulnerable, in support of each other during times of grief and mourning.[9] Adolescents often have multiple technology options to contact others, have been reared on technology, and comfortably turn to the digital world following news of tragedy or death.

Regarding social media's integration into daily life, Jed Brubaker and his fellow researchers provide the perspective that although Facebook is regarded as too insouciant for weighty issues such as death and grief, it does provide people with opportunities to engage with fellow mourners and the deceased in multiple ways unlikely in traditional grief practices such as funerals and memorial ceremonies.[10]

Brandon Ambrosino has described Facebook as a "growing and unstoppable digital graveyard," predicting that at some point there will be more deceased users than living ones.[11] He describes the phenomenon of our deceased loved ones being kept alive by their continuing presence as "strange." He continues that Facebook

---

7. Stillman, "Virtual Graveyard," 49.

8. Stillman, "Virtual Graveyard"; Brubaker et al., "Beyond the Grave"; Jones, *Dwell*; McEwen and Scheaffer, "Virtual Mourning"; Bourdeloie, "Digital Lives"; Walter, "New Mourners."

9. Gilbert, "Death, Grief"; Sofka, "Net Generation," 47–57.

10. Brubaker et al., "Beyond the Grave."

11. BBC, "Digital Graveyard."

transforms the experience of death and mourning as distant digital servers hold and maintain thoughts, images, memories, and relationships. He contends that these public digital records serve as our digital souls that continue to exist after death: displaying personal views, reservations, likes, and dislikes. Some user pages are "memorialized" upon notification to Facebook; others are not and can become unsettling to some as "digital ghosts," serving as continual reminders of loss and death. Bourdeloie warns that unless the bereaved act to remove their loved one's digital identity from Facebook, they would have to endure their digital persistence and may suffer the "violence of programmed algorithms" that cannot distinguish between deceased or live users.[12]

The emerging phenomenon of online interactions by the bereaved with their loved ones has resulted in various phenomena. These include memorialization, sharing and identity formation of the deceased, continuing bonds with the deceased, meaning-making, new death practices and rituals, addressing the dead, techno-spirituality, and new opportunities for therapeutic responses to death and mourning.[13]

MEMORIALIZATION

Digital platforms such as Facebook facilitate memorialization through digital cemeteries and web memorials. Facebook profiles have become unintentional memorials, allowing death to be drawn into everyday life in ways that non-digital memorials do not.[14] Jeffrey Bennett and Jenny Huberman refer to the paradigm shift away from traditional lavish funerals to cheaper and less traditional ways of memorializing the dead, as the "memorial paradigm shift from monuments to megapixels."[15] They refer to the former as burgeoning at the start of film photography (c. 1860)

12. Bourdeloie, "Digital Lives," 5.
13. Doughty et al., "Current Trends."
14. Ebert, "Profiles of the Dead."
15. Bennett and Huberman, "From Monuments to Megapixels." Quoted from abstract.

Outlining the Emerging Phenomenon

and the latter becoming ascendant with the advent of the digital era (c. 2000).

Walter explains that in the 1990s, the first generation of online memorials (virtual cemeteries and web memorials) brought social, demographic, and technological changes for mourners.[16] After the 2000s, there were significant changes for mourners' social relationships, comparable to the changes brought by urbanization and industrialization, due to the user content generated by SNSs and its "mobile-technology-enabled pervasiveness."

Kimberly Hieftje describes the deceased's Facebook profiles as personal memorials, used for celebrating their lives, remembering the good times, and keeping memories alive.[17] Logistically, instead of travelling to a memorial such as a gravestone or finding a photo album, a Facebook profile as a memorial is accessible at any time, from anywhere. Such a profile remains indefinitely, providing a place for friends and loved ones to feel connected to both the deceased and their significant others.

IDENTITY OF THE DECEASED

Traditionally wakes, funerals, candlelight vigils, and obituaries (oral and written) were ways in which the deceased's identities were constructed and maintained through narratives concerning the deceased. Digital technology and presence have presented new identity formation and maintenance opportunities, occurring both intentionally and inadvertently. Intentional digital identity formation is produced by adding memories, narratives, images, and information to existing Facebook user accounts or creating memorialized pages for mourning after the death of a loved one.

As mourners post messages, tags, images, or information to the deceased's Facebook page that may or may not be biographical, their identity expands and is modified. Jo Bell and coauthors propose that the online identity alters and evolves after death as

16. Walter, "New Mourners."
17. Hieftje, "Role of Social Networking," 39–43.

new aspects of a person often emerge.[18] Brubaker and company argue that creating or adding narratives and expanding identity can assist in the bereaved's grieving process and enables continued bonding activities.[19] SNSs such as Facebook cut across different social contexts and add narratives that may even be conflicting in nature, thus assisting in reconstructing a collective memory or identity of the deceased.

The dynamic nature of Facebook contributes to new issues around identity, such as conflicting or alternative narratives, symbolic ownership, digital legacy, and management of postmortem digital identities. Brubaker and coauthors state that adding new posts can produce tension for Facebook "friends" over content deemed as "inappropriate" or "inauthentic," conflicting values, questionable digital etiquette, "oversharing," opposing religious themes, alternative bereavement narratives, and the question regarding managing (or not) of new comments.[20] Brubaker et al. and Walter argue that arriving at a singular identity becomes problematic through this collective process of identity formation. As the number of contributors increases, so does the potential for tension and divergence.[21] Luke Van Ryn and his coauthors agree and found that as contributors with different relationships with the deceased added to the dialogue in polyvalent contributions, the memorialization became fragmented. It becomes problematic to unify into a cohesive narrative about the deceased.[22]

CONTINUED BONDS

Digital interaction between the bereaved and the deceased's online presence and identity through sharing and identity formation activities enable continuing bonds between the living and the

---

18. Bell et al., "We Do It to Keep Him Alive."
19. Brubaker et al., "Beyond the Grave."
20. Brubaker et al., "Beyond the Grave."
21. Stillman, "Virtual Graveyard"; Walter, "New Mourners."
22. Van Ryn et al., "Researching Death Online."

deceased. Bell and coauthors describe this process as Facebook connecting the past with the present but argue that whilst it has potential benefits in helping during the grieving process, it may also present potential overdependence on the continued relationship.[23]

Heidi Ebert believes that the deceased creator of the Facebook profile remains socially alive through their continuing presence as "an active agent in the lives of others."[24] Thus, Facebook activity creates a platform for social interaction by offering opportunities for the construction of autobiography and enabling both memory making and mourning, functioning as shared spaces that facilitate relationships between the bereaved and their deceased loved ones.

Hieftje describes continuing bonds with the deceased as "a dynamic, ever-changing process that includes constructing an inner representation of the deceased into the lives of the living" that may change over time, sometimes more active or passive, but the connection with the deceased remains intact.[25]

MEANING-MAKING

Mourners are left to interpret both autobiographical and biographical content such as expressed views, comments, images, and other materials of the deceased and understand this fusion to preserve the deceased's identity, which can be helpful in the process of making sense of loss.

Meaning-making, the process of reassessing and reviewing one's sense of how the world works, is central to the process of grieving after a loss. Participating as a mourner on an SNS such as Facebook may expedite the meaning-making process through connection with others and the deceased during a time of grief.[26] Sofke and company agree that sharing perspectives and unique viewpoints about the meaning of death with others, in the process

---

23. Bell et al., "We Do It to Keep Him Alive."
24. Ebert, "Profiles of the Dead," 24–25.
25. Hieftje, "Role of Social Networking," 40–41.
26. Hieftje, "Role of Social Networking," 41–45.

of meaning-making, helps to validate those perspectives and the meaning of death for others.[27] New digital platforms help bereaved individuals make sense of their loss through connectedness and constructing the deceased's identity.

FORMING COMMUNITIES FOR GRIEF AND MOURNING

Walter explains grief experience from a sociological perspective in four stages: (1) community mourning (preindustrial societies)—people living close, with high child and infant mortality rates that connect people as co-mourners; (2) private mourning (twentieth century)—grief becomes privatized as death becomes "medicalized" in hospitals and nursing homes, and co-mourners become supporters.[28] Bereaved mourners are isolated in their grief, searching for help in counseling, pastoral care, therapy, and mutual help groups as grief becomes "psychologized"[29]; (3) public mourning (late twentieth/early twenty-first century)—celebrity culture and pervasive mass and online media contribute to controversial public mourning of public figures; (4) online mourning—pervasive and user-generated mourning heralds the return of community mourning and memorializing as social relationships bring private experiences of grief out in the open. People publicly communicate what they feel in private. The bereaved become co-mourners again, able to connect from everywhere at any time.

Facebook serves as a form of thanatechnology for users choosing to bond with others over the death of a loved one in existing interactive communities for a sense of belonging in their grief, providing a comfortable space for sharing their death and bereavement experiences. Gilbert agrees that mourners will likely seek support and connection from their existing social networks. Although people experience grief privately, social engagement

27. Sofka et al., "Thanatechnology," 4.
28. Walter, "New Mourners."
29. Walter, "Different Countries"; Walter et al., "Die and Mourn."

Outlining the Emerging Phenomenon

with others over a similar experience helps develop a "confirmatory system," helping to form a healing narrative for the bereaved that is part of the grieving process.[30] Stillman suggests that the ability of mourners to connect on Facebook implies three vital points.[31] Firstly, users assess others' grief experience concerning the deceased to validate their relationship with them. Secondly, the deceased's social networks on Facebook are crossed and linked through the creation of a mourning community that shares a similar death event. Thirdly, it implies the "fractal nature" of individuals as mourners try to reconstruct whom the deceased was by searching for more information based on what other mourners share, thereby acknowledging that few, if any, knew the deceased fully.

NEW DEATH PRACTICES AND RITUALS

Digital technologies have changed the way mourners grieve as the physical constraints of time, social access, and geographical location are removed. Brubaker and his coauthors state that the "temporal, spatial, and social constraints" of traditional death practice and mourning rituals such as funerals, wakes, and candlelight vigils are removed through these technologies.[32] Mourning, memorials, death narratives, and rituals are opened to almost anyone as the private (and constrained) becomes public (and unconstrained). The use of virtual cemeteries, flowers, candles, lanterns, condolences, and online memorials have sprung up. Online ordering of caskets and flowers, and online arrangement of funerals are available and growing in some countries. Online memorial pages and groups have rapidly multiplied. Thanatechnologies have encouraged the formation of mourning communities among the bereaved in a way that traditional rituals cannot. Temporary communities may occur at or after funerals, wakes, or vigils, but

30. Gilbert, "Death, Grief," 295–97.
31. Stillman, "Virtual Graveyard," 50.
32. Brubaker et al., "Beyond the Grave."

periodic graveside communities are unlikely to form and remain. These technologies have enabled new rituals in regular interaction in online mourning communities.

ADDRESSING THE DEAD

Jed Brubaker and Gillian Hayes highlighted an interesting phenomenon found during their research in another SNS called "Myspace" that no longer exists. They found that mourners almost exclusively addressed their comments to the deceased.[33] This phenomenon is also found on Facebook, where directly addressing the deceased continues to dominate communication relating to death and the afterlife.[34] Lusi Castro and Victor Gonzales, and also Erinn Staley, discuss the implied assumption by the mourners that the deceased is "real," even without a physical presence, and can somehow receive the messages directed to them, although they do not deny their death. Castro and Gonzales describe a Facebook profile as a presence perceived as always being "on," ready to receive messages, "a surrogate presence of the physical one."[35] They argue that this surrogate presence can be perceived as more "real" after death as it is no longer just a means of staying in touch but "becomes the object of communication."

TECHNOSPIRITUALITY

Technospirituality or "digital religion" refers to another emerging phenomenon found in postmortem postings in the ubiquity of technospiritual practices. Jed Brubaker and Janet Vertesi, Jimmy Sanderson and Pauline Hope Cheong, and Erinn Staley found religious language, terminology, references, symbols, and discourse

33. Brubaker and Hayes, "We Will Never Forget."
34. Bourdeloie, "Digital Lives"; Castro and Gonzales, "Afterlife Presence"; Gilbert, "Death, Grief," 299–302; Hutchings, "Death, Emotion and Digital Media"; Staley, "Messaging the Dead," 12–15.
35. Castro and Gonzales, "Afterlife Presence."

Outlining the Emerging Phenomenon

to be comingled with the popular and are becoming mainstream practices, surprisingly not confined to extreme faith-based communities during times of death and mourning.[36]

References and implications of an afterlife are pervasive in messages posted to Facebook profiles of the deceased. Staley proposes three beliefs about the afterlife found in such postings:[37]

1. the ability of the deceased to receive electronic communication.
2. the deceased is in heaven.
3. the living user and the deceased will somehow be reunited one day.

There seems to be no expectation of receiving messages back from the dead. Sending such messages to the deceased is generally accepted practice and ritual practiced by many as they effectively keep the memory of their loved ones alive. Staley suggests that one could ask if these practices imply replacing or modifying Christian theology regarding mortality and the afterlife but contends that the users' belief that the dead are removed to "up there" and not nearby, coupled with no expectations of receiving communication from the deceased, indicates no such controversy.[38] Through the comments expressing reuniting the live and deceased someday, eschatology's conventional Christian ideas as "future and otherworldly" are continued and facilitated as mainstream.

THERAPEUTIC APPROACH

Grief, loss, and bereavement are part of the human experience. Walter described the twentieth century as the advent of the "psychologizing" of mourning, where grief became privatized, and mourners felt increasingly isolated from their social networks. Such privatization and isolation drive mourners to seek help from

---

36. Brubaker and Vertesi, "Death and the Social Network"; Sanderson and Hope Cheong, "Tweeting Prayers"; Staley, "Messaging the Dead."
37. Staley, "Messaging the Dead," 14–15.
38. Staley, "Messaging the Dead," 16–17.

caring professionals and mutual help groups.[39] These help groups started moving online in the 1990s, providing easy, accessible, and timely help at anytime from anywhere.

During this period of "professionalizing" death and mourning, there was a move towards the pathologizing of grief.[40] Leeat Granek mentions three serious consequences of this pathologizing effect:

1. placement of unrealistic expectations on mourners in terms of presentation and duration of grief, resulting in shame and embarrassment when these expectations are not met by the "psy-disciplines."
2. movement of treatment towards "medicalization" through antidepressants, antianxiety medication, and sleeping pills.
3. pressure on mourners to seek professional help instead of their established social supports, making their experience even more private and isolating.

Alternative grieving rituals and the move towards finding support in community have spontaneously emerged, seen in the construction of public shrines after the death of Princess Diana, at the sites of the September 11 terrorist attacks and the Oklahoma City bombing, and especially in the proliferation of digital mourning sites and online grief resources. Granek describes this as an "electronic grieving phenomenon," a growing "counterculture" seeking community and collective grieving in online memorial spaces.[41] Walter describes this as moving back towards the preindustrial village mourning practices where communal support was found in close social connection.[42]

The dominance of traditional grief theories, literature, and assumptions such as the phase or stage models, most notably the

39. Walter, "Different Countries"; Walter, "New Mourners"; Walter et al., "Die and Mourn."
40. Granek, "Is Grief a Disease?," 266–75; Walter, "Different Countries"; Walter, "New Mourners"; Walter et al., "Die and Mourn."
41. Granek, "Is Grief a Disease?"
42. Walter, "New Mourners."

Outlining the Emerging Phenomenon

Kubler-Ross stage model, Freud's "grief work" model, and others, have implied universality of the grieving experience.[43] Those beliefs are changing. Current research shows that grief and loss experience is unique, individual, and dependent on many variables and contains multiple and multifaceted reactions that include physical symptoms.[44] The acceptance of multiple theoretical orientations has led to mental health professionals adapting and practicing a variety of models and adaptations to help their clients. These include:

- the acceptance of the need for continuing bonds by some.
- a greater understanding of attachment theory and its role in thanatology.
- applying the dual process model that combines elements of other models.
- constructivism that emphasizes multiple truths organized by the mourner in finding meaning.
- adaptive grieving styles, reflecting mourners' individual cognitive behaviors and affective strategies for adaptation to loss.

From the discussion it is clear that the digital world has increasingly seen new phenomena in grieving, mourning, memorializing, and expressing technospirituality through SNSs such as Facebook. Research and scholarship over the past two decades have produced fascinating data, concepts, opinions, recommendations, and controversy.

---

43. Kübler-Ross, *On Death and Dying*; Breen and O'Connor, "Fundamental Paradox"; Doka, "What's New in Grief?"; Doughty and Hoskins, "Death Education."

44. Doughty et al., "Current Trends"; Doka, "What's New in Grief?"

2

Comparing Traditional Caucasian Euro-American and Digital Bereavement Practices

RITUAL: WHAT IT IS

Catherine Bell and Pamela Stewart and Andrew Stratham highlight renewed recent interest in ritual as a topic of interest and scholarship and not merely a tool used to understand the culture.[1] Ritual has changed over centuries and particularly over the past twenty years. Bell states that it was initially regarded as a tool to describe and elucidate religion and its influence for many. Later it became a tool to explore ritual activities in order to analyze and interpret cultural understanding of them. Today, ritual is understood by many to be fundamental to the dynamics of culture. Bell proposed the concept of "ritualization" as a way of "doing" rather than a "thing," as processes that are brought into being to transform the "doing" or acting with an authoritative character in order to move or shift in a direction. Stewart and Stratham regard ritual as a constant in an ever-changing world, "affording a space for reflection, to slow down time, to restore order, or to assert,

---

1. Bell, *Ritual Theory*, 3, 13–14; Stewart and Stratham, *Ritual*, i–iii.

transform, and reassert identities."[2] Stewart and Stratham have described the characteristics of ritual as implying "formality, regularity, stereotyping, special uses of language and communicative gestures and sanctions concerning its correct performance."[3] They agree with Bell in describing it as not being a "thing," but rather as a term for methods or processes and events within social life.

RITUAL: WHAT IT DOES

An important question to ask is, "What does ritual do?" Bell contends that it appeals to tradition through its often exact repetitions of earlier activities. However, it can adapt to new circumstances or even recreate something new while evoking elements from past activities, thus inventing new traditions that can express cultural-historical patterns for mourners.[4] William Hoy asserts that funeral rituals provide a sense of calm, inner balance, and order for both the bereaved and the community during the chaos of a loved one's death.[5] Rituals help the bereaved to make sense of the mysteries surrounding death. Although funerals have changed over the past two centuries in Western culture from the expensive, lavish Victorian funerals of the late nineteenth century to the inexpensive, less lavish, and more nontraditional memorial services we often see today, it is digital technology that has changed the landscape of traditional death and bereavement rituals and practices and the way mourners cope with loss.[6]

2. Stewart and Stratham, *Ritual*, iii.
3. Stewart and Stratham, *Ritual*, 1–3.
4. Bell, *Ritual Theory*, 145–51.
5. Hoy, *Do Funerals Matter?*
6. Bennett and Huberman, "From Monuments to Megapixels."

RITUALS AND PRACTICES: COMPARE AND CONTRAST

From the proliferating, emerging phenomena of digital interactions between the bereaved and the online presence of their loved ones, it is clear that many death, grief, and bereavement rituals remain similar in form (funerals, wakes, and memorialization remain). Nevertheless, these are different in how they "look," how long they last, and what they "do." Virtual funerals are watched repeatedly by many, online, in a private experience, then shared and communicated by many, crossing social boundaries with communication and recordings becoming memorialized.

Van Ryn and company recently concluded that digital ethnography is made up of various ontological layers interconnecting in many ways but found that social media does not merely "sit on top" of existing mourning and memorializing practices or rituals.[7] Their study found that digital ethnography "appropriates, extends, and transforms those practices."[8] Digital activity is not only "in addition to" existing practices of death and commemoration. Such activity has the ability and potential to change and transform. These are the arguments made by academics like Bell, Stewart and Stratham, and Bjorn Nansen and coauthors.[9]

Physical and digital rituals display some apparent similarities in form but present with contrasts and differences in appearance and function. Some differences appear to be more subtle, and others are vastly different. Physical rituals such as funerals, wakes, cremations, and memorials provide a heightened visual and an experienced reality for attendees that is usually only experienced once (unless recorded) and is also experienced by fellow attendees. These physical ritual events enhance the ideas and beliefs around the deceased's physical, biological, social, and final death. An interesting phenomenon at physical spaces for ritual (such as

---

7. Van Ryn et al., "Researching Death Online."

8. Van Ryn et al., "Researching Death Online," 14.

9. Bell, *Ritual Theory*; Stewart and Stratham, *Ritual*; Nansen et al., "Restless Dead."

cemeteries) is the hybrid interfaces that are commencing where media, through sounds and digital images, are "bringing to life" the deceased in what Nansen and company call the "restless posthumous existence" of the deceased.[10] In contrast to physical rituals, virtual streamed funerals, wakes, cremations, and memorials present diminished visual and experiential effects for mourners watching online on digital platforms. These mourners can watch the recording multiple times in private. The deceased remain digitally alive and "present" to mourners, and their social presence remains interactive and dynamic: temporal and animated. In a temporal sense, their presence and the communication surrounding them present as mundane, transient, and secular, unmediated by the religious or sacramental, effervescent due to the "sensory and emotional stimuli." Their social presence remains "animated" in the sense that it is active, engaging multiple mourners, and offers hundreds and even thousands of words and digital images.[11]

Nansen and company describe physical spaces for ritual such as cemeteries as a geographical and material location and focus for more permanent mourning.[12] Loved ones design gravestones, epitaphs, and obituaries after careful consideration. These people make the items from durable materials meant to last for decades and even centuries. Conversely, digital memorial spaces, their digital "counterparts," provide mobile locations and a focus for mourning. These spaces are materially impermanent and have become increasingly mobile with the onset of mobile "smart" devices. These "inscriptions" and memorial contributions are informal, authored by many (close and loose associations), dynamic, unlimited, temporal, and animated. Such things provide a platform for the digital augmentation of everyday physical artifacts such as photos and other images for fellow digital mourners to view, interpret, and discuss.[13]

10. Nansen et al., "Restless Dead," 111.
11. Hutchings, "Wiring Death"; Hutchings, "Death, Emotion"; Nansen et al., "Restless Dead," 111–24.
12. Nansen et al., "Restless Dead," 111–24.
13. Hutchings, "Death, Emotion"; Nansen et al., "Restless Dead."

Physical rituals often refer to the spiritual afterlife. Digital rituals provide the basis for both the digital and spiritual afterlife of the deceased.[14] References to the expectations of a spiritual afterlife of the deceased are made extensively on SNSs and other digital platforms. Studying these references, Staley found three persistent beliefs expressed on digital platforms: (1) the deceased receive digital messages; (2) the deceased is in heaven; (3) the deceased will be reunited with their loved ones in the future.[15]

Technology and digital communication are returning death from its previous sequestered locale back into daily life, providing emerging and alternative ways of living with death, grief, and bereavement. New practices and rituals are brought into our everyday living spaces through SNSs and the digital world. Walter and his coauthors concur and state that SNSs and the internet have vastly changed death and mourning practice by making it interactive. These authors use examples of virtual attendance and live streaming of funerals, online help groups, digital memorials, and more.[16] Their study finds that "grieving with strangers has become a common tradition" and a "collective experience."[17]

SPIRITUALITY, RELIGION, AND RITUAL PRACTICES

Religion and ritual have historically been closely connected.[18] Religion has served as a significant and meaningful source of comfort and consolation at times of significant loss, specifically in the area of death and bereavement. Funerals, wakes, and memorial services were traditionally mostly held with Judeo-Christian religious practices for Caucasian Euro-American practice. Neil Thompson

---

14. Briggs and Thomas, "Social Value," 133–34; Staley, "Messaging the Dead," 13–14.
15. Staley, "Messaging the Dead."
16. Walter et al., "Die and Mourn."
17. Walter et al., "Die and Mourn," 276.
18. Bell, *Ritual Theory*; Stewart and Stratham, *Ritual*; Hollenback, "Ritual and Religion"; Thompson, "Role of Religion," 337–49.

writes that religion provides stability and guidance through its familiar religious frameworks and predetermined beliefs during the profoundly destabilizing experience of grief.[19] Religion legitimizes certain practices and rituals, justifies actions, and provides an individual and social dimension to addressing existential questions relating to death, grief, and bereavement. These preset religious beliefs provide a framework for behavioral expectations that can guide mourners in their actions, thoughts, and feelings.

The sociologist Malcolm Hamilton makes a critical yet arguable point about the average mourner and religious ritual practice:

> To understand religion, one has to analyze first and foremost what people do and not what they believe. Practices are primary and beliefs secondary. This is why beliefs are often rather vague, inconsistent, and contradictory. People are not so much concerned about doctrine but with rituals and observances.[20]

Others would argue that mourners would have to accept and embrace as truth the preset religious framework of beliefs for it to be an honest agent for comfort, solace, and positive change. Thompson agrees and states that when working with mourners, one would have to understand or at least have a degree of awareness of their religious beliefs and background. It is not good enough to categorize someone as "religious" or group them into "religions." One individual may experience their faith very differently from another, even from within the same religion.[21]

Although religion is a significant foundation of spirituality, it is not the only source. Spirituality, described by Thompson as "the sense of meaning, purpose, and direction," which may or may not be derived from religion, is becoming an increasingly important social phenomenon.[22] According to Thompson, everyone has spiritual needs and experiences spiritual challenges that may heighten

---

19. Thompson, "Role of Religion."
20. Hamilton, *Sociology of Religion*, 109.
21. Thompson, "Role of Religion."
22. Thompson, "Role of Religion," 337.

during death and bereavement. Stillman proposes that SNSs such as Facebook provide fertile ground for meaningful spiritual experiences and interactions. Many researchers such as Brubaker and Vertesi, Sanderson and Hope Cheong, Staley, and more have highlighted the emerging phenomenon of *technospirituality*.[23] Furthermore, Stillman and Lorne Dawson refer to cyberspace as a continuation of real life where spiritual activity is mediated online and where "cyberspace becomes sacred space."[24]

Dawson makes some interesting points regarding religion, faith, spirituality, and cyberspace, and highlights two emerging problems: authenticity and authority.[25] He claims there is much ambiguity regarding spiritual concepts and terms and the representation thereof. Are the posters (on Facebook) or digital content creators authentic in whom they claim to be or represent? Do they understand the organization they claim to represent and are they genuinely aligned? When they refer to "holy," "angels," "heaven," "god," "God," "hereafter," "Christian," "church," and more, what is their understanding? What is the correlation between their online and offline religious or faith-based practices? Is their cyber-religiosity authentic? Dawson cautions against anyone making their "religious" or spiritual claims known to an unlimited number of readers. They may not rightly represent what they claim and could cause unease for the reader.

Spirituality has recently received attention in thanatology, sociology, education, psychology, counseling, and pastoral and spiritual care. Thompson identifies six areas of spirituality that are impacted by experiences of death and significant loss:[26]

1. Meaning: central to spirituality and loss in forming narratives to guide thoughts, feelings, actions, and interactions.

---

23. Stillman, "Virtual Graveyard"; Brubaker and Vertesi, "Death and the Social Network"; Sanderson and Hope Cheong, "Tweeting Prayers"; Staley, "Messaging the Dead."
24. Stillman, "Virtual Graveyard," 47; Dawson, "Religion and the Quest."
25. Dawson, "Religion and the Quest."
26. Thompson, "Role of Religion," 344–47.

2. Purpose: everyone faces the quest for finding purpose in the "why" questions.
3. Direction: grief often causes "biographical disruption" and may remain, or a new direction may be found—also known as "transformational grief."
4. Connectedness: serving as a sense of solace in finding connection with others.
5. Awe and wonder, or "the numinous": often negated temporarily but may be found in renewed compassion or "humanness" through significant loss experience.
6. The sacred: easily understood in religious form but can be attached to grieving individuals and their needs, burial sites, and more.

Ritual practices surrounding loss, death, and bereavement of traditional Caucasian Euro-American people have changed over time by becoming less expensive and elaborate, less religious, and more fluid and accepting of change. However, the greatest changes have emerged with the digital age's advent over the past two decades. Death and bereavement have been catapulted back into public life, practiced in an online community, and memorialization has changed from the temporal to the "eternal." Issues such as digital estates and legacies, management of online interactions and ownerships, digital etiquette, lurking "digital ghosts" and their impact, online grief help groups, funeral planning, virtual funerals, online eulogies, and online memorials have become the norm. These things continue to evolve as interactions increase and disciplines such as thanatology, entrepreneurship, education, psychology, theology, and more become involved.

3

Bereavement, Embodiment, and Cybergnosticism

Foundational Issues

Are online bereavement, grief-related technospirituality, and digital memorialization cybergnostic? Has Gnosticism evolved here into a form of cybergnosticism? It is essential to ask this question, lest caring professionals fall into the trap of encouraging an unhelpful disembodied and dualistic faith and spirituality. Chapter 3 examines Gnosticism of the second and third centuries and its key features and ideologies to make this assessment. Chapter 4 goes deeper, concentrating on Gnosticism's views and practices, online bereavement, and digital memorialization. These viewpoints relate to human personhood, community, and engagement with the world and social performance.

The definition of Gnosticism and gnosis has not been an easy task for scholars. A committee of scholars at an international conference on "the origins of Gnosticism," held in Messina, Italy, in 1966, wrestled through to the following thoughtful definition:

> The Gnosticism of the second-century sects involves a coherent series of characteristics that can be summarized

as the idea of a divine spark in man, deriving from the divine realm, fallen into the world of birth and death, and needing to be reawakened by the divine counterpart of the self in order to be fully reintegrated. Compared with the conceptions of a devolution of the divine, this idea is based ontologically on the conception of a downward movement of the divine whose periphery (often called Sophia or Ennoia) had to submit to the fate of entering into a crisis, and producing—if only indirectly—this world, upon which it cannot turn its back, since it is necessary for it to recover the pneuma—a dualistic conception on a monistic background, expressed in a double movement of dissolution and reintegration.[1]

The committee was also concerned about distinguishing *Gnosticism* of the second and third centuries from *gnosis* by defining gnosis as "knowledge of the divine mysteries reserved for an elite."[2] In this definition, gnosis as a concept covers the knowledge mentioned above and also the broader movements characterized by such knowledge or "gnosticizing ideology,"[3] which certainly predate and exist independently of (or interdependently with) Christianity. The origins of such gnosticizing ideology include Platonism, Alexandrian philosophy, Zoroastrianism, and other Persian philosophies, and possibly, though contentiously, the Buddhism of India.[4] We follow the Messina methodology, using *Gnosticism* and *gnostic* with specific reference to "classical" gnostic systems of the second and third centuries while appreciating that *gnosis* might be applied much more broadly to movements and ideologies preceding and following this era.[5]

---

1. Bianchi, ed., *Origins of Gnosticism*, 26–27.
2. Bianchi, ed., *Origins of Gnosticism*, 26.
3. Arai and Ariarajah, *Spirituality in Interfaith Dialogue*. Quoted in Wilson, "Slippery Words," 298.
4. Renwick, "Gnosticism," 485.
5. Rudolph criticizes this distinction since in his mind "gnosis" and "Gnosticism" is the same thing, but we will carry on the Messina delineation for clarity of terms. Rudolph, "'Gnosis' and 'Gnosticism,'" 57.

Given the complexity and dense terminology surrounding discussions about Gnosticism, which is partly due to the complexity of gnostic theologies, we will seek to provide a brief explanation of the main ideas in the Messina definition of Gnosticism. We present here the ten key ideas within the Messina definition, with a clarification of each.

FIRST: "A coherent series of characteristics . . ." The Messina definition, then, agrees with authors such as Kurt Rudolph, Pheme Perkins, and Hans Jonas that an overview of early Christian Gnosticism is possible through a consideration of its coherent and principal series of characteristics.

SECOND: "Summarized as the idea of a divine spark in man (sic), deriving from the divine realm, fallen into the world of birth and death . . ." This is a central idea in the Gnostic myth. Human beings have a soul that has been created by the evil powers of the world (hence their passions, desires, and instincts), and they also have a spirit (a divine spark) that has been given them by the highest God and derived from the divine realm. This spirit is imprisoned by the evil powers of this world in human bodies and is thus "fallen into the world of birth and death."

THIRD: "Needing to be reawakened by the divine counterpart of the self in order to be fully reintegrated." The spirit (or sparks of light and particles of *pneuma*) within human beings is reawakened by gnostic knowledge and through an encounter with the divine, and redemption happens when these sparks are freed from the imprisonment of the world and the body and are collected together and brought back to the highest God, from which they came, and reintegrated into God.

FOURTH: "A devolution of the divine . . ." This means that the divine is fractured, decentralized, and convoluted. "Devolution" should be understood as a movement downward rather than an evolutionary movement upwards or forwards. There is a rupture within the divinity itself, a cosmic accident or fall, and the world and human beings come into existence because of this fatal rupture. How does this cosmic accident happen? The highest God's mirror image takes on an autonomous existence and becomes a new being, lower than the highest God, yet also a part of God (she is often called Sophia). This begins a differentiation within the divine. From Sophia, the gnostic mother goddess emanates a sequence of divine graduations, and these graduated "powers" are often called "aeons." These beings are not contrary to or of a different substance than the highest God, yet they are not quite he, for they are a "devolution" of God. Thus, the highest God is not responsible for the creation of material or earthly things.

FIFTH: "This idea is based ontologically on the conception of a downward movement of the divine . . ." The divine splinters into various beings, of the same substance as God, but not exactly God. Lower divinities (such as the Old Testament God) are therefore responsible for evil, matter, the creation of the world, and flesh.

SIXTH: "Whose periphery (often called Sophia or Ennoia) . . ." Sophia is the perfect aeon (or the divine graduation and being who is most like the highest God), yet she is not the highest God. She is the gnostic mother goddess and is sometimes called Barbelo. It was from her transgression that the world and all matter was created, if only indirectly.

SEVENTH: "(Sophia) had to submit to the fate of entering into a crisis, and producing—if only indirectly—this world . . ." From Sophia comes (emanates) the God of the Old Testament (or Ialdabaoth, the "Demiurge" in gnostic literature), who creates human beings and the world. This theology allowed the gnostics to maintain a negative view of creation and matter and reject the Old Testament's God. Material and earthly things are the responsibility of the Old Testament's inferior God (the

Demiurge), who happens to be ignorant of his inferiority, and the highest God stands apart from these things.

EIGHTH: "Upon which it cannot turn its back, since it is necessary for it to recover the pneuma..." The highest God chooses to correct the error of Sophia and the Demiurge, however, by reflecting Godself in human form in the waters of the lower heavens, so that the Demiurge (the Old Testament God) unknowingly and through a fascination with the form reflected in the waters decides to create such a being. The highest God then tricks the Demiurge into imparting some of the pure light (pneuma) he has received from Sophia into human beings so that they may live. The Demiurge is not the only one to possess the particles of light (pneuma), which he had stolen from the heavens through Sophia. This potential element of the divine can be brought back to the highest God (its origin) through human beings. This divine spark within human beings can be reintegrated with the divine through secret knowledge and gnostic enlightenment. This gnostic knowledge and enlightenment, therefore, is the path of salvation and redemption for human beings.

NINTH: "A dualistic conception on a monistic background . . ." There is proposed in gnostic theology an evil principle that stands alongside the highest God. The world and all things material are the product of this evil principle, and there is a cosmic struggle between these dual forces of darkness and light. Behind this dualism is a monistic conception of the highest God, who is eternal, immortal, unnamable, imperishable, immeasurable, perfect, and incomprehensible. This highest God is the genuine core and ultimate substance of all things. Although all things exist in God, this highest God is insuperably distant from the world and all of the created order. He thus originates Gnosticism's metaphysical dualism, which results in the gnostic repulsion toward the world, the body, and all matter.

TENTH: "Expressed in a double movement of dissolution and reintegration." There is a disbanding or fracturing that happens within the divine, and therefore within the universe, that is paralleled or resolved by reintegration of persons back into the divine through the gnostic enlightenment of the human person, and through reintegration of the divine sparks into the highest God.

Therefore, the Messina definition suggests that Gnosticism of the second-century sects involves coherent characteristics, summarized as the idea of a divine spark in humanity (the human spirit or *pneuma*), which is fallen and imprisoned. This spirit needs to be reintegrated with the highest God, who is its source. The highest God has fractured into various beings, of the same substance as the highest God, but not precisely God, and the most perfect of these is Sophia, from whom comes the God of the Old Testament (the Demiurge). Sophia commits an error of judgment that allows the Demiurge to create all things material. The highest God must restore the divine spark within human beings to Godself, through the redemption of human beings from all things corrupted, embodied, and material, through gnostic knowledge and enlightenment. Such gnosis, then, is the source of human and cosmic redemption and salvation.

PHILOSOPHICAL AND THEOLOGICAL UNDERPINNINGS OF GNOSTICISM OF THE SECOND AND THIRD CENTURIES

With the Messina definition established, we now consider the general philosophical and theological underpinnings of second- and third-century Gnosticism. We then examine gnostic considerations about human personhood, community, and engagement with the world and social behavior. The sources used in this examination include the scholarly considerations of persons such as Hans Jonas, Alastair Logan, Elaine Pagels, Birger Pearson, Perkins, Rudolph, and English translations of the church fathers, apocryphal hermetic writings, Mandaean and Manichean writings, and the Nag Hammadi texts.[6]

We use the sources we have mentioned to examine the key themes of the second- and third-century gnostic movements such as Valentinianism, Basilideanism, Saturninianism, and Marcionism. There were four distinct movements within Gnosticism of the first to third centuries AD. (1) The Valentinians were the most influential and important school within Gnosticism of the second century AD, and they originated from the gnostic philosopher Valentinus (born around 100 AD). He taught that the Demiurge created the world and that a whole genealogy of several generations of aeons existed instead of one Son. (2) Basilides founded the Basilideans. He was noted for teaching that the world is continuously evolved from a *panspermia* or germinal "seed of the world" where all things find their origin. (3) Saturninus of Syria, who was a heavily dualistic and gloomy, material-hating ascetic, led the Saturninians. For Saturninus, the God of the Hebrews was only an angel, and the Son did not have a real body, marriage was a base adultery from the first love of God, and eating meat was an indulgent sin. (4) The Marcionites were a product of the vision of Marcion, who condemned the God of the Old Testament and drew up his gnostic canon of Scripture. He was fervently ascetic and condemned all Christian connections with the world and with matter.

Michael Waldstein, in order to construct the overarching gnostic myth, quotes Jonas, who views Gnosticism and its mythology as a story from the unitary principle *Entweltlichung*, located within seven patterns of transition or schemata, that "form a system that tends toward what Jonas calls 'the foundational Gnostic myth.'"

---

6. See bibliography for the details of the works of Jonas, Logan, Pagels, Pearson, Perkins, and Rudolph that were consulted in this study of Gnosticism. See also: Jonas, "Return to the Divine Origin"; Jonas, *Religious Context*; Hedrick and Hodgson, eds., *Nag Hammadi*; Hultgren and Haggmark, eds., *Early Christian Heretics*; Robinson, ed., *Nag Hammadi Library*.

> [T]he distance of the world from God (the schema of distance); the enclosure of the world (the schema of the dwelling place or cavern); the imprisonment of human beings in the world (the schema "far down" or "here"); the experience of being lost (the schema of the labyrinth or of multiplicity); the self that does not belong to the world (the schema of negativity or point-like isolation); God as utterly above the world (the schema "high up" or "outside" or "there")—in addition, orientations of movement implied in all these schemata and constitutive of their unity: fall, sinking, loss of the origin and the reversal of all these in an inverse process (the schema of movement down or up or of becoming distant and returning).[7]

Gnosticism, therefore, was characterized by a profound dualism and alienation that governs the relationship between human beings, the world, and God. The highest God is entirely other, unknowable through the wisdom or speculation of humanity, in no way resembling the substance of the cosmos. The highest God "neither created nor governs [the world and cosmos] and to which it is the complete antithesis: to the divine realm of light, self-contained and remote, the cosmos is opposed as the realm of darkness."[8] The world's creation is the result of a tragic indiscretion by the lower Sophia who vainly attempted to produce an offspring like the Mother without a consort or the approval of the highest God, and her product was an abortion—the ignorant, arrogant Demiurge (the Old Testament Creator God).[9] The Demiurge, the archons, and the inferior rulers created the world and obstruct human beings from access to and proper knowledge of the One and of salvific gnosis, which requires supernatural enlightenment and illumination.

Furthermore, in gnostic thought, the cosmos and the human body are restrictive prisons, conspiring to separate humans from God. Gnostics desired esoteric knowledge and freedom from the

---

7. Jonas, "Gnosis Und Spatantiker Geist," 362–63.
8. Jonas, *Gnostic Religion*, 42.
9. Logan, "At-Onement," 485.

world's constraints and oppression. They pursued freedom from what they considered "flesh-shaped" and "unspiritual" theology, cosmology, anthropology, eschatology, and morality. The desire for mystic knowledge also shaped their Christology, which in turn had a profound effect on their concepts of human personhood, the world, ethics, and community:

> Called to awakening and repentance from this world of exile and oblivion, and granted the saving knowledge, he/she is then baptized in the threefold name of the Gnostic triad, Father, Mother, and Son, and anointed as a Christ in the mysterious right of the five seals marking the descent of the Spirit. He/she is thereby called to live a life of ascetic denial of the world and its hostile powers and structures, including sexual division, the material body, fate and astrology and even the worldly systems of justice and morality—all the creation of the Demiurge (the "prince of this world") and his archons—until death and the return to the unknown God.[10]

Gnosticism of the second and third centuries was a mixture of gnosticizing movements represented by the above-mentioned well-known groups, which engaged vigorously with Christianity and threatened the distinctive nature of many canonical, church-sanctioned doctrines and behaviors. Church leaders responded theologically and with a deep sense of urgency about the dangers of gnosticizing ideologies and theologies.

EMBRACING EMBODIMENT AND SALVATION

Gnostic anthropology held an elite claim to superior, enlightened knowledge critical for true human freedom and salvation. According to the gnostics, this is because gnosis is a requisite to salvation (as opposed to faith or the observance of the law), and since true knowledge of self and the Divine is salvific knowledge. The Messina definition of Gnosticism describes this theology as "a divine spark in man (sic), deriving from the divine realm, fallen into the

10. Logan, "At-Onement," 485–86.

world of birth and death, and needing to be reawakened by the divine counterpart of the self in order to be fully reintegrated."[11] This reintegration through gnostic knowledge leads to salvation and redemption. This entails an eschatology that reserves salvation for those with gnosis and ultimate destruction for the cosmos and the minions of the cosmos. According to Gnosticism, nothing material may be redeemed or saved.

Gnostic salvific theories and models tend to oversimplify human need, distort Scripture, and reshape the narrative contours of salvation that the Christian theological tradition presents. Christians believe that salvation is deeply rooted in human history, profoundly relational, and mediated through the person and work of Christ. Salvation is incarnationally orientated, mutually defined, and outworked (by the human and the Divine), and eschatologically hope-filled. The experience of Jesus Christ as Savior—not salvation through some unique acquisition of knowledge—lies at Christianity's heart and origins. Christians need to rediscover embodied, Christ-centered salvation in the twenty-first century. Enfleshed faith guards against gnosticizing trends.

Salvation and human flourishing are not primarily ideas or theological concepts. They are the experience of grace that transforms a person's whole life. Salvation is embodied, practical, and social. Salvation may also be considered holistic healing (rather than a mind-centered adoption of secret knowledge) and a way to fullness of life and human flourishing (in the person and work of Christ). Salvation is the restoration of people to communion with God, with each other, and with creation. Our common need for redemption and salvation comes from personal sin and systemic and societal evil and oppression. We need salvation because we have become captive to personal sin and structural oppression. Our relationships with God, self, others, and creation are broken without Christ. We need the healing power of Christ's truth and love. Authentic other-centered living, inner healing, and holiness lend credibility to Christ-centered salvation.

11. Bianchi, ed., *Origins of Gnosticism*. See also Newman, "Theology and Science," 40.

The message of salvation in Christ is holistic. By holistic, we mean that salvation is about body and spirit; peace with God and people and creation; healing, forgiveness, reconciliation, liberation, and freedom. Salvation is physical and spiritual. This redemption is for whole persons, whole communities, whole churches, whole neighborhoods, the whole world, and the whole creation. It is a message of God's shalom offered to all people, the whole creation, and the entire cosmos. God in Christ Jesus saves, restores, and transforms all things material and spiritual. This is a radically different message than the gnostic focus on "secret knowledge" and "immaterial and esoteric spirituality." In Christ, God invites us to participate in the liberation and restoration of all things: spiritual or material, eternal and temporal, mystical and embodied.

EMBRACING LOVE AND RELATIONSHIP

Human beings are relational and yearn for identity, love, purpose, and meaning. These things are the evidence of both the *imago Dei* and the presence of divine grace. Our identity and relationality are sourced in God's creation of our beings and our formation in God's image. God's grace fulfills the human yearning for destiny and hope. The desire for more than this life offers, the frustration of the inadequacy of things acquired and achieved, and the radical protest against death are the human yearnings for grace and redemption.

This urge is essentially a relational one, and much human suffering is the direct result of alienation and isolation. Human beings are interpersonal, relational, and intersubjective at their core. We are created in the image of a relational God who enjoys perfect relationship, love, and communion within the Trinity. Humans are invited into this relationship, and communion with the Divine and with other persons is the means of salvation, healing, and fullness of life. This communion extends into the interconnectedness of people with all things nonhuman. We are subject to the consequences of our actions upon the same. The flourishing and interconnectedness of humanity with God is inseparable from the flourishing, well-being, liberation, healing, and relatedness of all creation. Our bodies, nature, and all creation are related. Humans are thoroughly connected with the social, political, and economic structures and institutions of the world; and depend on the ecological systems of the planet. We are subject to the consequences of our actions in these areas. We, therefore, have a profound responsibility for that which God and humanity create, whether living or inanimate. Human beings are essentially relational. We yearn for genuine community. The gnostic extremes of asceticism, disembodiment, hyperspirituality, spiritual elitism, and dualism are unhelpful.

EMBRACING OUR PHYSICAL-SPIRITUAL, BODY-SOUL UNITY

Within Gnosticism, there is a dualistic perspective on the relationship between matter and spirit. Gnostics consider matter evil and corrupt. They believe that evil is sourced in matter and that the cosmos (and the human body), having been created by an inferior Demiurge, is a dungeon in which human souls are held captive. The highest God is not responsible for the perversion that is material things, therefore. The Demiurge is the source of matter, creation, and evil. This Demiurge is the creator of the world and matter, is quite distinct from the Deity, and is identified with the God of the Old Testament. The Old Testament God is considered inferior and remote from the Supreme Being. The highest God removes Godself from all things material. The Demiurge, who is the world's inferior creator, is responsible for the Old Testament, the Law, all created things, and evil itself. From this understanding of the Christian God and God's relationship to all things material emerges a docetic Christology that denies the full humanity of Christ. Gnostics deny the literal suffering and crucifixion of Jesus Christ. The Supreme God (who is not the Old Testament God) is understood as impersonal and incapable of physical suffering. The supreme and highest God removes Godself from the matter and substance of the world. Therefore, according to the gnostics,

Christ must not have had a literal body, been fully human, or been bodily crucified and resurrected.

Gnostic theology is a syncretistic combination of Christian, Platonic, Alexandrian, Zoroastrian, Persian, and possibly Indian Buddhist philosophies and theologies. Gnosticism is a "distinct religious movement, or cluster of movements, attested in history; that is to say, one can speak of 'the Gnostic religion' as a discrete historical phenomenon, distinct from, even if closely related to, Judaism and Christianity." However, Gnosticism is highly parasitical, growing substantially out of and away from Judaism, and intricately engaged with the Christian tradition.[12] However, its perspectives on the human body, matter, creation, and the participation in these things by the Divine, are at odds with the Christian view.

We compare these theological foundations in Gnosticism with Christian theology in greater detail here since this area is critical to our study of digital memorialization and online bereavement ideas and practices. Gnostic understandings of the relationship between matter and spirit (matter as evil and spirit as good) are critical to gnostic and gnosticizing theologies.

Human beings, in Christian theology, are created beings. The Genesis account describes human beings as being created by God in God's image, as sexual and embodied creatures. We are not self-sufficient. We are profoundly relational. We are formed from "dust," not as a closed historical event but as a process. Not only are we fashioned from "clay" by our Creator at our conception, but our entire lives are also a testimony to the process of renewal, physicality, embodiment, and creative Divine genius. To be a creature is to be shaped by God from nothing and be birthed into a process of being called and created. God calls us to fulfill our God-ordained purpose: glorifying and praising God through matter, physicality, spirituality, and embodiment. We are continually being created and so are firmly located within the created order. Nicholas Lash, in *Believing Three Ways in One God*, writes: "What makes the doctrine of createdness good news is the discovery that

---

12. Pearson, "Eusebius and Gnosticism," 292.

Bereavement, Embodiment, and Cybergnosticism

God makes the world 'parentally.'"[13] We humans experience the parental nature and extravagant love and pleasure of God in our createdness and embodiment.

God continually forms and sustains creation parentally. Human beings are a part of creation, enjoying the filial care and concern of the Creator Father. Humanity, though at times deluded by visions of grandeur and self-sufficiency, is not self-made. We are continually created out of the abundance of God's immeasurable love and grace. Humanity, formed by God and located within the world, is interdependent. We do not merely share the origins of other created things but are woven into the fabric of the created order in mysterious and inexplicable ways.

We share the realities of gender, reproduction, embodiment, and sexuality with other living creatures. Like other living things, these elements of sexuality and embodiment are subject to physicality, ecology, abuse, power, social and gender relationships, genetics, and time and space. Our sexuality, relationality, and physicality proclaim our location within the created order. This embodiment is a mirror of the web of relationship that all created things share. So, the pathological urge to live as "nonsexual," disembodied, spiritual beings or, conversely, to indulge in hedonistic, immoral, and self-indulgent lifestyles is to deny the relational essence of our matter. God calls us to live within the communion and fullness of life that God the Father offers in Christ through the power of the Spirit. Both hedonism (self-indulgence) and extreme asceticism (denying the body) are dualistic, failing to appreciate our relational embeddedness and embodiment in creation.

As created beings, the created order (the "world") is the theater in which our lives unfold. We experience sexuality, work, family, commitments, spirituality, politics, society, suffering, ecology, achievement, failure, and joy in the body. Religious and spiritual movements have moved between the poles of sensual deification and the repulsion of all things "unspiritual." Religions have too often sought to enable adherents to escape the worldly realities of birth, death, body, sexuality, and human society.

13. Lash, *Believing Three Ways*, 43.

In Christ's incarnation, humans are affirmed as created beings. The created order is honored, as God comes into our created context to redeem and heal, affirming the intrinsic value of created matter and humanity. In the incarnation, Christ reveals his ongoing relationship to creation, including humankind. Christ also shows a willingness to engage with the contours of creation, being time, space, and matter. Human nature, essence, and physicality are liberated, honored, and graced by Christ and his incarnation. As part of creation, we experience grace, freedom, personal dignity, and the source of our inner yearning. In assuming human form, God declared creation to be good, embodiment to be desirable, humanity to be of intrinsic worth, and salvation and human flourishing to be located in our humanity, our relationality, and our bodies.

There is, therefore, a theological and "earthly" unity between the realities of creation and incarnation, in which we freely share. God's ongoing creative activity and incarnational presence sustain a Christ-dependent world. This world is in a real relationship with the Divine, even though the Creator is radically distinct from it. God is in an ongoing relationship with creation, which includes humanity. An existentially dependent creation, including humanity, is not independent of its Creator. Humans (and all creation) are recipients of God's ongoing creative processes, goodness, love, and presence. Thus, humanity, as part of creation, gives glory to God.

The Creator's glorification is the creation's ultimate purpose—along with relational, non-subsumed union with the Trinitarian God. Our purpose, along with all creation, is to glorify, praise, and exalt our Creator—and all creation does this materially and spiritually. The history of creation—past, present, and future—is the place where God reveals God's glory, love, presence, and plan. Humanity, as part of creation, is destined to glorify God along with the rest of creation.

As beings that are essentially part of creation, we share the history of God's salvific relationship to the world along with the rest of creation. As creatures made in the image of both God and creation, uniquely charged with its care, we are to treat the rest of creation with the profound honor that reflects how our identity, physicality, and destiny are enmeshed with it and redeemed along with it. Human beings do not exist in transcendent, subduing, monarchical relationship to the rest of creation. As part of creation, humanity participates, communes, communicates, loves, repents, and breathes in the mysterious interrelationships of the created order. We find salvation and divine life through the incarnational presence of God in this embodied and physical realm.

A gnosticizing dualistic, utilitarian, and subjugating understanding of creation is nonsense. Such theology or ideology is self-destructive, as human history testifies (e.g., nuclear proliferation, ecological genocide, unconscionable genetic experimentation, pandemics, loss of biodiversity, and global warming). We cannot escape the consequences of our actions toward the rest of the created order precisely because humanity is a part of creation and because God freely engages in a loving relationship with creation.

Since humanity is part of creation, Christian theological anthropology sees an interdependent connection between world, body, and history. Humans are embodied in skeletal, muscular, respiratory, nervous, and cardiovascular systems (to name a few) as created beings. Our embodiment is in the world (we are immersed in structural and systemic realities—political, economic, social, religious, and more). The theater upon which we experience this drama is physical and historical (time, space, matter, the realm of the spirit, and living organisms interweaved in a cosmic drama since the creation of the world).

Since this is the case, dualism is in vain. The body and the soul are one. The body is enlivened and given form by the soul, and the soul finds expression and spiritual completion through the body. Consequently, humanity as a soul/body unity is located ontologically in the world. There is no other arena in which human beings, in God, "live and breathe and have their being" (Acts 17:28). To delude other human beings by encouraging them to neglect the body and deny goodness within society through gnostic-like religious doctrines and practices is damaging and dangerous (possibly even blasphemous). Gnostic ideology denies people the opportunity to live fulfilled and prosperous interpersonal, embodied, and fully human lives.

As inextricably part of creation, human beings are soul and body within history and society. This existential and fleshly unity is consubstantial, an active rather than passive dynamic. Spirit and flesh enrich, complement, and complete each other in human history.

To compel human beings to see themselves as conflicted entities in constant battle with their corrupted and corrupting flesh—or as spiritual beings needing freedom from the body and the world—is to deny the goodness and wisdom of the Creator. To do so is to see the creation as innately flawed, conflicted, and debased. This perspective denies creation, incarnation, crucifixion, and resurrection.

We have examined the general philosophical and theological underpinnings of Gnosticism. Our focus in the next chapter becomes more specific and deals with human personhood, community, and engagement with the world and social behavior.

4

Bereavement, Embodiment, and Cybergnosticism

Specific Issues

Our consideration now concentrates on gnostic views of personhood, community, and engagement with the world and society.

GNOSTIC PERSPECTIVES ON PERSONHOOD

Gnosticism of the second and third centuries maintained a distinct tripartite concept of the human person, which resulted from gnostic mythology. Though it has some variations in the various gnostic schools, the gnostic anthropological creation myth focuses on the paradise story of Genesis 2–3. This myth unravels, in its barest possible form, in the following way. The supreme God acts to correct the error and indiscretion of Sophia by reflecting his image in human form in the lower heaven's waters. The Demiurge and the archons are so taken by this image that they decide to create such a being. The archons of the seven authorities each contribute to the soul of the human being. The angels of the highest God fool Ialdabaoth into imparting some of the pure light into Adam so that he lives. Now those particles of light can return to their origin through the redemption of human beings. These humans also have a soul and trace elements of the divine spirit (a divine spark), which make them superior to the powers of the cosmos.[1]

The four archons then employ matter through the four elements of the world and passions, instincts, and desire to imprison and entomb the soul-spirit in a body. All of the human psychic and material components are fashioned by these archons, beginning with the head and working downward, as detailed in the *Apocryphon of John*:

> The first one began to create the head: Eteraphaope-Abron created his head; Meniggesstroeth created the brain; Asterechme the right eye; Thaspomocha the left eye; Yeronumos the right ear; Bissoum the left ear; Akioreim the nose; Banen-Ephroum the lips; Amen the teeth, etc.[2]

The gnostic myth then proposes that demons and archons are assigned to rule over the different senses, the passions, and the emotions. A destructive, rebellious spirit, hostile to God, is implanted in human beings by the four archons to contradict and work against the divine spark. A woman is created from Adam by the Demiurge to possess and wield Sophia's power. Sexual desire is fostered in the human heart to cause them to struggle against and contradict the divine spirit.

Therefore, a tripartite concept of the human person is maintained. The body is a tomblike prison. The world's evil powers create both the body and the soul with all of their passions, sexual desires, and instincts. The spirit (spiritual seed or divine spark within) is the only part of humankind that retains the divine spark of light that may return to the highest God. The spirit, then, is the

---

1. Williams, *Rethinking "Gnosticism,"* 119.
2. "Apocryphon of John," 15:29–17:31, pp. 107–9.

Bereavement, Embodiment, and Cybergnosticism

only thing that is of any value in a human. The spirit is the only thing capable of being redeemed and saved.[3]

Since the soul is the seat of human passions, gnostics devalue the soul along with the "prison" of the body. The spirit within is exalted as the source of enlightenment and the bearer of the divine spark. However, not all human beings maintain a similar relationship between the body, soul, and spirit, since persons are either "pneumatic," "psychic," or "fleshly" ("earthly" or "material").[4] Paul the Apostle uses the same tripartite approach in his theological anthropology—spirit (*pneuma*), soul (*psyche*), and body (*soma*). Whereas *soma* refers explicitly to the body, when Paul uses the word *sarx* (flesh), he often refers to the whole, unregenerate person. Therefore, *sarx* should not be considered synonymous with *soma*.

Jonas quotes Irenaeus as confirming that according to the Valentinians: "There are three kinds of human beings, the pneumatics, the psychics, and the material, like Cain, Abel, and Seth; they use these three biblical figures to demonstrate the three natures, not in the individual human being, but in the human race as a whole."[5] While the psychics' fate (those Christians focused on the psyche/soul) remains in the balance, the fleshly (those Christians and non-Christians controlled by the soma/body/flesh) are headed for destruction. Only the elite, spiritual, enlightened pneumatics (those Christians dedicated to the pneuma/spirit) are unquestionably preserved for salvation. These spiritual elite seek to convert the ordinary Christian from a mere psychic experience of the divine, which is tenuous and dangerous, to an exalted pneumatic encounter with God that leads to salvation. Through their mystical, secret knowledge, the pneumatics are convinced that they have experienced far more than the psychic Christian. Psychic Christians need to be freed to pneumatic awareness, higher forms of worship, a mystical experience of the One, and a gnostic

---

3. Jonas, *Religious Context*, 467–70.
4. Edwards, "Neglected Texts," 30–31.
5. Irenaeus, "Against Heresies 1.7.5," 469.

certainty of salvation. They need freedom from lower, degenerate levels of awareness and communion with God.[6]

Humans live, then, with the tension between matter and spirit. The person's soul may either proceed upwards through participation in the spiritual or move downwards through a desire for the material, fleshly, and earthly realm. Sophia stands at the intersection of this polarity. This gnostic anthropology explains the presence and tension of the divided self. Only through *gnosis* can one become fully integrated and progress upward toward the Divine and God's liberation. Some of the Nag Hammadi Scriptures describe an enthronement that is yet to be unveiled. This enthronement happens as the soul ascends through the spheres and receives an unction.[7] The coming of the true human is coupled with gnostic enlightenment and illumination and anointing with the unction of the life eternal. Such an experience is only available through the pathway of *gnosis*.

The human body and its physiological processes are also used analogously for describing and considering themes in gnostic theology, cosmology, soteriology, and sociology. Since the physical body is contrary and opposed to the spiritual spark within humans, gnostics used it to symbolize negative cultural, anthropological, and structural processes and rulers on varying levels. Since the body entombs the spirit and makes it numb to the Divine's presence and purposes, it is used negatively in its embryological, morphological, and cosmological symbolism.[8] According to Ingvild Saelid Gilhus, "the orifices of the body and their discharges are the marginal points of the system. It is—like every structured system—vulnerable at its margins, and those marginal areas are seen as especially dangerous." The female physiological processes are especially used in "the negative evaluation of theology, cosmology, society, and material existence."[9] Gnostics viewed the

---

6. Pagels, *Johannine Gospel*, 120–21. For Logan's defense of some of these perspectives and fervors see Logan, "Truth in a Heresy?," 191.

7. Robinson, ed., *Nag Hammadi Library*, 38.

8. Gilhus, "Gnosticism," 111.

9. Gilhus, "Gnosticism."

female reproductive organs, sexual desire, and human instincts and impulses as created by the Demiurge to prevent human beings from pure and redemptive *gnosis*. Gnostics despised the products and intimacies of sexual intercourse and human sexuality. They used the metaphor of birth to describe the cosmos' creation as a gross product of birth.

In Gnosticism, the sexually compelled human body and soul are filthy, repulsive, entombing prisons. The soul and body are a body of darkness and a beast.[10] *The Treatise on Resurrection* pronounces, "The afterbirth of the body is old age, and you exist in corruption."[11] The body, then, is reflective of and connected to the hierarchical order of the archons. The body is a perverse and frustrating cage for the human spirit, the divine spark within the human person.

This gnostic theological anthropology embodies the dualistic gnostic tension between spirit and matter. This anthropology has profound implications for how gnostics constructed their theologies of creation, Jesus, and salvation. It also impacted their approach to ethics, since if the body is depraved, imperfect, and evil, what does it matter how one uses or abuses it? This leads to extremes of asceticism and licentiousness among gnostic practitioners and schools.

Gnostic docetic Christology is closely linked with these perspectives on the human person and the body in Christian Gnosticism of the second and third centuries. The Christ needed only to have a spiritual body—an *ochema*, the semblance of a body, made of a pneumatic substance—that allowed him to descend to the world of flesh.[12] A variation of this idea is found in the gnosticizing "separation" Christology, enabling them to propose that the spiritual Christ unified with the human being Jesus of Nazareth for the period between the baptism and the crucifixion. Jesus, the man, left behind his undesirable body as the heavenly Christ returned to the supreme God. In both instances, the gnostics denied the

10. "Apocryphon of John," 116; "Paraphrase of Shem," 339, 347, 357.
11. "Treatise on the Resurrection," 52.
12. Quispel, "Original Doctrine," 343.

embodied and enfleshed elements of the incarnation, perceiving them as repulsive and incredible. The concept of Christ's actual physical death on the cross is rejected and eliminated. The salvific role of the crucifixion is seriously undermined and supplanted by the quest for gnostic knowledge.

So, we have the following gnostic texts denying the full, embodied humanity of the Christ, and rejecting his "fleshly" parts, just as gnostics portray the human body as doomed, dangerous, deceptive, undesirable, and unworthy:

> Sometimes, when I made to touch him, I encountered a material, firm body; another time, when I touched him, the substance was immaterial and unbodily, as if it did not exist.[13]

> "John, as far as the crowd down there in Jerusalem are concerned, I was crucified and pierced with lances and reeds, and given vinegar and gall to drink. But now I am talking to you . . . I am not the one on the cross . . . thus I have not suffered any of those things that they will say about me."[14]

> "I did not die in reality, but in appearance . . . [I]t was another, Simon, who bore the cross on his shoulder. It was another on whom they placed the crown of thorns. But I was rejoicing in the height . . . And I was laughing at their ignorance."[15]

> "He whom you saw on the tree, glad and laughing, this is the living Jesus. But this one into whose hands and feet they drive the nails is his fleshly part, which is the substitute being put to shame, the one who came into being in his likeness."[16]

For the gnostic, then, the human person is tripartite. Only the divine spark or spirit is worthy and can experience salvation

13. *Acts of John*, 93.
14. *Acts of John*, 97–101.
15. *Second Treatise of the Great Seth*, NHC VII/2, 55:18–19, 56:9–14, 18–20, in Robinson, ed., *Nag Hammadi Library*, 332.
16. *Apocalypse of Peter*, NHC VII/3, 81:15–23, in Robinson, ed., *Nag Hammadi Library*, 344.

by an ascent to the heavenly realm and the supreme One, and reintegration into the divine, through immersion in *gnosis*.[17] This kind of theology seriously weakens the public nature and responsibility of faith. We see this undermining of public witness in the gnostic views on community and social behavior.

GNOSTIC VIEWS ON COMMUNITY

The writing of the church fathers confirms that Gnosticism of the second and third centuries was located in various schools or sects. The existence of gnostic writings themselves confirms that there must have been gnostic communities behind these texts. These communities would have maintained some form of ecclesiology or understanding of the community and the church's nature.

The gnostics, however, were generally opposed to any formal manifestation of a social system. Enthusiasm for liberation from the inferior soul, rejection of the human body as undesirable, and repulsion toward the perceived binding social constructs of the church and the world and their rulers led to the development of a liminal, loosely connected fraternity within gnostic sects. These communities formed around simple social structures with functional leadership and mystical perspectives on interconnectedness. They denied formal hierarchies, at least in theory. These gnostic communities not only stood in opposition to existing and "corrupted" social structures—aside from when they were accommodating Hellenistic culture for their purposes and gain—but also formed their meaningful *communitas*.

Gilhus suggests that "The anti-structure of Gnostic *communitas* is revealed in its antinomian character, be it as freedom from or rebellion against the Law; in the violating of family-ties, either in the form of absolute asceticism or as promiscuity; and in the abolishment of status-distinctions. *Communitas* is established on the principle of equality within."[18]

---

17. Pearson, "Gnosticism as Platonism," 67–68.
18. Gilhus, "Gnosticism," 119.

A pneumatic-charismatic-organic formation of each gnostic community stood in contrast to the relational and hierarchical order they perceived in the church. A gnostic group that stands in contrast to this general model is the Manicheans, whose structures were developed and hierarchical. The Manicheans maintained a distinct division between the *electi* (perfect) and the *auditores* (hearers).

Jonas proposes that the two main models of *communitas* or *thiasos* the gnostics followed were the cultic and mystery associations and the philosophical schools.[19] Gnostics formed these associations, groups, and schools for the following purposes: (1) to distinguish themselves from the existing church and religious institutions; (2) to prevent an overarching organization from coming into existence; (3) to provide a basis for interpersonal exploration of the mysteries; (4) for participation in unique forms of worship, sacraments, prayer, and cult; (5) to secure a location for a community of fellow pneumatics dedicated to achieving *gnosis*; (6) to develop rituals, initiation rites, and necessary self-organization to sustain their movements; (7) to permit loose gatherings based on specific needs and situations; and (8) whether social, ministerial, or missiological, to decide what activities were needed and acceptable at any given time.

The Christian gnostics did, infuriatingly for their opponents (especially for the Christian church leaders and teachers), see themselves as Christians. These gnostics adopted the *ekklesia* concept as they depicted themselves as the true elect, the *pneumatics*, the only genuine and solely chosen and sanctified "church" in the world.

Tertullian is particularly damning of these communities. However, some of his polemics give us insight into the egalitarian, anti-hierarchical, participatory, and experiential nature of these communities. Even their negative analogous use of femininity and the female anatomy seems to be overridden by their commitment to the full participation of the pneumatics regardless of

---

19. Jonas, *Religious Context*, 487.

their sexuality (and sometimes because of their sexuality, suggest Robert Grant and Jorunn Buckley):[20]

> Nor will I omit a description of the manner of life of the heretics, portraying it in all its looseness, its worldliness, its low human character, without dignity, without authority, without church discipline, and utterly in keeping with their own faith. To begin with, one does not even know who a catechumen is and who is a believer. They go in together, they listen together, they pray together . . . All are puffed up, all promise knowledge. The catechumens are already *perfecti*, even before they have received any instruction. And then, the heretical women—how impertinent and presumptuous they are! They take it upon themselves to teach, to engage in disputes, to carry out exorcisms, to promise healings, perhaps even to baptize too . . . Nowhere is promotion easier than in the camp of the rebels, where mere physical presence counts as virtue. So one of them is a bishop today, another tomorrow; someone is a deacon today and a lector tomorrow; or else, a priest today and a layman tomorrow. For they entrust the priestly functions to laymen too.[21]

However, those who participated in these gnostic communities were gripped by a consciousness that focused on individualism and on "individual transcendence."[22] For the Gnostic, a personal sense of calling did not need to be validated by the community or any other existing institutions. Gnostics held a deep conviction that it is I who is *pneumatic*. The gnostics believed they knew this because of an intensely personal and experiential revelation to oneself. Gnostics believed an "encounter with Christ is a recognition of one's own hidden, unknown true identity . . . the discovery of self . . . (which is an) experience to be actualized."[23] Gnostics coupled this experience with a concern for a personal reward for

---

20. Grant, "Gnostic Spirituality," 54–55; Buckley, "Libertines or Not," 17–21.

21. Tertullian, "Prescription," 487.

22. Perkins, *Gnostic Dialogue*, 10.

23. Green, *Economic and Social Origins*, 215.

one's gnosis and spiritual status, both in this life and the one to come. This reward was in the form of sensory pleasure or illumination and mystical and metaphysical personal transformation.

Gnostic individualism evidenced an absence of a personal obligation to the Mosaic law, the church's ethical or social teachings, and the state's political and social institutions. Gnostics expressed their individualism through autonomously determined and critiqued freedoms and ethics, which they often expressed in highly individualistic and self-selected libertinism or asceticism.

Gnostics also believed that it is the assertion of the individual's will and effort that moves one from the status of *material* or *psychic* to *pneumatic*. They also proposed that people achieve salvation from determinism (fate) and to illumination by working out their own redemption and self-realization. "Only by living to the full his (sic) human adventure was the Gnostic able to realize his (sic) dream of freedom."[24] Jonas writes that "The immediate illumination not only makes the individual sovereign in the sphere of knowledge (hence the limitless variety of Gnostic doctrines) but also determines the sphere of action."[25] Elaine Pagels maintains that "Only on the basis of immediate experience could one create the poems, vision accounts, myths, and hymns that Gnostics prized as proof that one actually has attained gnosis."[26] These are valuable summaries of the grip of individualism and privatized spirituality on second- and third-century Gnosticism.

Therefore, Gnosticism's perspectives on community were both a reaction against the institutionalism and formalism of the existing church and other Hellenistic religious institutions and a manifestation of anti-cosmic and highly individualized mythological paradigms. Their individualized and privatized spirituality equally matched their organic, participatory, experiential, and decentralized expressions.

Therefore, Gnosticism evidenced a range of community expressions and approaches to social ethics. Gnostics expressed these

24. Filoramo, *History of Gnosticism*, 189.
25. Jonas, *Gnostic Religion*, 46.
26. Pagels, *Gnostic Gospels*, 145.

social behaviors and ethics through asceticism as a means of intimate connection with God and licentiousness due to indifference to human ethics or the laws of the Demiurge of the Old Testament. Gnosticism's social, ethical, and ritual dimensions were held together by its complex, syncretistic, and evolving mythology. Each gnostic teacher added to these dimensions so that these myths and communal rituals became highly complex and rigorous.

GNOSTIC OPINIONS ON ENGAGEMENT WITH THE WORLD AND SOCIETY

Gnostics believed the lower Old Testament God created the world and the cosmos. Sophia's indiscretion and deviance (she is not herself the highest God) caused a fatal rupture within the divine. This cosmic accident or fall brought about the birth of human beings and the world through Ialdabaoth, the lower and perverted creator God of the Old Testament. Ialdabaoth created the world in ignorance of his limitations and smallness in comparison with the Supreme God.

The following gnostic quote describes the creation of the Old Testament God by Sophia. Sophia herself is not the highest God but the one who is closest to him. The section explains how gnostics could attribute the world's creation to an inferior and evil being (the Old Testament God, who they often called Ialdabaoth). The quote also shows how gnostics reserved spiritual, good, and perfect things to the highest God (sometimes called the *Pneuma* by the gnostics).

> Our sister, the Sophia, being an Aeon, conceived a thought, and through the thought of the Pneuma and Prognosis, attempted to project from herself the Image. The Pneuma (the Highest God) had not approved and had not given her permission, nor her Partner and Consort, the male Virginal Pneuma . . . Her thought could not remain ineffective, and her work emerged imperfect, and ugly in appearance, since she had produced it without her Consort . . . She saw that it (the Old Testament

God) was different in form, having the appearance of a snake and a lion. Its eyes streamed fire. She cast it (the Old Testament God) away from her, outside of those areas, so that none of the immortals might see it, because she has borne it in Ignorance. She bound it in a cloud of light and set a throne in the midst of a cloud . . . She gave it the name *Ialdabaoth*.[27]

In this way, the gnostics explained their negative view of the created world and its structural and social constructs and their rejection of the Old Testament concept of God as perverted and evil. While this explains the mythological basis for the gnostic suspicion of the created world, its powers and its material, we now must explore how the gnostics regarded engagement with or participation in the world. We also explore what level of social interaction and involvement the gnostics saw as desirable and how they felt compelled to behave morally and practically in society.

Michael Allen Williams, in *Rethinking Gnosticism*, argues that the gnostics maintained a much higher level of social participation and cultural engagement than has usually been proposed.[28] The four main arguments Williams suggests in support of this contention are listed here, along with some responses.

First, these supposed "anticosmics" may not have had a "calculated indifference or marked antipathy toward the Roman order" since many of them voluntarily choose to live and immigrate to the city of Rome.[29] This fact suggests they were not utterly hostile to political culture. This suggestion is certainly a significant one, although proximity does not equal engagement or participation. The gnostics indeed shunned the value of social engagement and secular involvement in the process of personal salvation and redemption.

Second, Tertullian of Carthage complained that those who leaned toward "heresies" socialized too much with worldly or culturally influential people. He lamented that their general conduct

---

27. "Apocryphon of John," 36:16–38:14, p. 104.
28. Williams, "Anticosmic World-Rejection?"
29. Williams, "Anticosmic World-Rejection?," 101–2.

was too earthy and on the human level. They too readily appointed people of public office or obligation to roles in leadership. They did not clearly distinguish between those who were full believers and those who were outsiders. However, we may interpret this charge by Tertullian as Williams does or as Tertullian's concern about the lack of respect from "heretics" (including gnostics) for conventional social orders and authority structures since they devalued these social concerns and systems acutely.

Third, Irenaeus of Lyons charged the Valentinians and Basilideans of indulging in food offered to idols, celebrating pagan festivals, and enjoying murderous spectacles between animals and gladiators. Williams suggests that this is evidence that they did not withdraw entirely from the world but engaged with it. Irenaeus's accusation, however, may also be evidence of gnostic libertinism and extravagant violation of traditional religious concerns and norms. Gnostics held little respect for the body and little regard for conventional Christian ethics.

Fourth, the widespread gnostic devaluation of martyrdom demonstrates that they were "advocating the toning down of Christian sociopolitical deviance."[30] Yet this unwillingness to suffer for a more significant cause and desire instead to engage in nonthreatening philosophical pursuits may show a Gnostic disregard for "material" or "physical" expressions of faith.

Williams writes that we can explain the incongruence between the seeming accommodation of Hellenistic culture and tradition and the rejection of the material world and its structures by this fact:

> Not all, and not even some of the most interesting, of the groups, figures, or texts that have conventionally been labelled "Gnostic" were in fact all that socially or politically deviant, on a scale of relative social or political deviance—and therefore are not best described as "anticosmic" or "world-rejecting" in any social or political sense.[31]

30. Williams, *Rethinking "Gnosticism,"* 105.
31. Williams, "Anticosmic World-Rejection?," 106.

Williams's last contention deserves significant recognition since it seems evident that gnosticizing ideology does not necessarily preclude one from an engagement in contemporary philosophical, cultural, and analytical concerns. Some gnostic groups maintained a significant and "anticosmic" distance from the prevailing Hellenistic culture, such as the Marcionites. Others certainly seemed to reconcile their philosophical dualism with their interest in social and cultural engagement through a tendency toward a lower level of sociocultural tension (examples include the Valentinians, Basilideans, the two Theodoti, and Natalius). The latter of these were able to justify this philosophically by claiming that participation in political and social forums was expedient for their cause and movement. Such participation was not threatening enough to rob them of their pure, higher, pneumatic state. It also allowed them to proselytize effectively, which the Valentinians and Basilideans were effective in doing.

These differing sociocultural tensions, participations, and concerns within Gnosticism explain the contradictory emphasis we see in gnostic social behavior and ethics. Libertinism and asceticism coexist in Gnosticism. The pneumatics, in the gnostic worldview, were utterly free from rigid external ties and obligations. Their bodies were mere vehicles for enlightenment and liberation. They were free to practice both indulgent libertinism and self-imposed asceticism as they saw fit and as best served the immediate needs of their "fraternity" and spiritual impulses.

The desire for full human experience compelled this existential approach to life and morality and an unrestrained immersion in the pleasures, struggles, and indulgences of life. This way, the Demiurge and his unnatural laws and restrictions would not control the pneumatic. Life separated from the world meant a life separated from the restraints and "perverse" boundaries of the world, hence libertinism. Yet, at times, it also meant a life given over to the sensual delights and fleshly concerns of the world, hence asceticism. Thus, gnostic groups concerned themselves with varying degrees of social accommodation and anticosmic alienation. The picture grows of groups that are not uniform or consistent.

The result is that Gnosticism offers no genuine systematic ethical constructs or guidelines for the adherent. This fact is not surprising given the gnostic view of this life's temporality and their soteriological emphasis on gnosis, which they did not define by conduct, obligation, or compulsion. The focus on gnosis also shaped the following: (1) gnostic understandings of salvation and which aspects of humanity are saved (i.e., the spirit); (2) their perspectives on the church's nature (i.e., spiritual and far from institutional); (3) the division between faith and practice, religion and ethics, and individual personhood and community responsibility.

Gnostic engagement with the world and society, therefore, seems to be centered on some essential things: an overarching disdain for the created order and its worldly structures; varying levels of sociocultural tension between gnostic groups; and opportunities for entertaining philosophical considerations and debate about contemporary social, political, religious, and cultural issues while renouncing the confines of institutional structures. Gnostics also emphasized the freedom to choose libertinism, asceticism, or something in between, based on one's gnostic journey. This individualized experience is also true of what moral and ethical perspectives a gnostic might choose for oneself.

FRANKENSTEIN AND OUR DIGITAL FEARS— SEEING PERSONHOOD, RELATIONALITY, AND EMBODIMENT DIFFERENTLY

We turn now to a story that will help us understand how we might respond to digital technologies (their positive and negative potentials) while avoiding Gnosticism's problems.

Mary Shelley's *Frankenstein*, also known as *The Modern Prometheus*, was written at a time much like ours. There were great fears and uncertainties about technological advances and how people would use them to enhance or degrade human life and society. The story is magisterial, with many layers of meaning. It serves as a warning about the dehumanizing potential of technology, about science gone too far, and about what happens when we dehumanize, alienate, and disregard vulnerable, hurting, marginalized people. In the story, the creature isn't the real monster. The monster is Victor Frankenstein. There are many lessons in this story for our understanding of online bereavement and digital memorialization.

We can give in to our digital fears. Or we can realize that the monster lies within us and our potential for abuse of peoples and technologies, not usually within the technology itself. We can accept the technologies uncritically, or we can engage with them ethically and compassionately. We can choose to be attentive to the grieving, mourning, isolated, and vulnerable. Shelley's *Frankenstein* calls us to see personhood, relationality, and embodiment differently than the gnostics did. We can value human dignity, fulfill the innate desire for community and relationship, and seek the ethical use of technologies and science. We can pursue human equality and care for those who are shunned or left behind. Shelley speaks to our use of technology, our digital fears, our understanding of humanity, and our efforts toward compassionate inclusion and genuine equality and mutuality.

Mary Shelley's progeny is Victor Frankenstein, a man plagued by four great existential mysteries: death, love, nature, and spirit (although Frankenstein seeks to evade the realities of these through isolation, compulsive work, god-delusions, scientific creativity, obsession with the "other," and vengeance). His inner turmoil haunts him in the guise of the creature, in his implicit captivation by death, in wearying creativity and activity, in his alienation from people and nature, and in perversions of authentic spirituality. Shelley comments on what it means to be a human person in this characterization. Shelley portrays the profound ambiguities, contradictions, and inconsistencies of human nature. For her, an existential crisis is multilayered, formational, and pervasive, manifesting itself in such perversions as self-deification and neglect of compassionate responsibility toward those who are vulnerable and that which is created.

The human propensity to create technologies without ethical consideration or care for whom they affect, and the human inclination to exalt oneself in a godlike fashion, and then avoid the consequences of one's egoism and self-delusion—these are vital themes upon which this novel turns. Victor Frankenstein represents the creative and often problematic faculties of human beings and the potentials of society. We have a fantastic potential for creating new technologies through science, especially in the digital age. But humans are given to ambition and greed, to lack of concern for the exposed, to god-delusions, and a misconception about the actual interconnections between the creator and the created. For Shelley, to be human is to have incredible potential for ingenuity. Yet to be human is also to be charged with profound responsibility for that which is created and released into the world.

The product or victim of Frankenstein's obsession is the creature. This creature begins life as benevolent and innocent, free from prejudice and malice, and moldable at the time of its creation. The creature's education and interaction with human society breaks his heart, alienates him, corrupts his instincts, and leads him to act despicably. He feels profoundly and desires relationship until those who find him repulsive, unfathomable, and "other" reject and abuse him. Shelley's understanding of the formation of the human personality, from innocence to adulthood, is relatively straightforward. Yet, she also portrays the interwoven destinies of the "creator" and the thing "created." The creature becomes the embodiment of Victor Frankenstein's repressed instincts, existential turmoil, sexual dysfunction, aggression, anger, and disaffection with human society. To be human is to have a dark side. To be whole is to come to terms with the same, moving beyond the alienation of irresponsible self-glorification to a meaningful and self-aware relationship with self and others. Shelley says that all technologies can express our darkest natures. But they can also present opportunities for ethical behavior and concern for the weak. They can offer opportunities to pursue equality and human dignity and enhance human flourishing. This is an apt parable for the digital age.

In Shelley's view, human beings often struggle with god-delusions while being blind to the consequences and responsibilities associated with their creations. At times, human beings endeavor to usurp the role of God. Such leanings toward self-deification are both a human dilemma and a source for astonishing creativity. Victor Frankenstein imagines how "a new species would bless me as its creator and source . . . No father could claim the gratitude of its child so completely as I should deserve theirs."[32] Mary Shelley suggests in her 1831 introduction that this is Frankenstein's major crime: the compulsion to displace God as the Creator.

Frankenstein's speech is an extraordinary expression of hubris. He is convinced that he, alone and unaided, could "pour a light into our dark world."[33] He, in isolated brilliance, would find the means to reject the work of death and, in so doing, enable others to participate in his deific transformation. Yet his passionate obsession is an evident displacement of normal emotions, healthy human relationships, genuine self-awareness, and appreciation of human limitations. In the perversions that result from this displacement, Shelley describes the needs and the shape of the human heart. Frankenstein's ardor for his deific experimental research makes him oblivious to the world around him, to his friends and family, even to his own constitution. As he admits, "my cheek had grown pale with study, and my person became emaciated with confinement" as "a resistless, and almost frantic impulse, urged me forward; I seemed to have lost all soul or sensation but for this one pursuit."[34] Rejecting normal human relations, he claims, "I could not tear my thoughts from my employment, loathsome in itself; but which had taken hold of my imagination. I wished, as it were, to procrastinate my feelings of affection, until the great object of my affection was completed."[35]

Victor Frankenstein substitutes the human need for emotional connection with a vision of personal omnipotence, to his peril, to the misery of his prodigy, and the terrible wrath of the scorned creature. This wrath's unleashing is placed within the

32. Shelley, *Frankenstein*, 55.
33. Shelley, *Frankenstein*, 55.
34. Shelley, *Frankenstein*, 43.
35. Shelley, *Frankenstein*, 44.

context of traumatic memory and experience as a significant source of the perpetration of (and inclination toward) evil. Cultural systems and technological advances (as macrocosms of interpersonal dysfunction) are critiqued as having the potential to transform victims of malignant trauma into perpetrators of these very traumas on others. The creature's catastrophic loneliness and self-hatred (a consequence of the trauma of personal rejection by his creator and by human beings and society in general) leads to the enactment of evil and the slide into perversity and spiritual degradation. Violence and alienation are birthed in Frankenstein's fervor for omnipotence and responsibility-free creativity rather than relationship.

Put another way, this evil is the result of Frankenstein's denial of innate human yearnings for identity, meaning, intimacy, purpose, and community. In his scientific fervor, he had gone the way of the gnostics, denying sexuality, embodiment, human dignity, and community. Frankenstein was a scientist, but while science concerns itself with the physical world, it often commits the same mistakes as Gnosticism. Frankenstein needed to take time to understand the nature of his creation and the human drive for embodiment, intimacy, equality, meaning, and worth. The same goes for the digital technologies we discuss in this book. The yearning for love and value are the sources of the monster's inner anguish. So, like online bereavement and digital memorialization, the creature became more than a symbol for the human drive for these things. Frankenstein was blind to this and paid the price. We must not do the same.

Human beings are profoundly relational. Much human suffering is the direct result of interpersonal alienation and the widespread denial of the relational interconnectedness of all things human and nonhuman. This alienation and denial often find roots in the idolization of the self (whether individually or corporately) and neglects personal and societal responsibility.

Frankenstein and the creature both suffer significantly from alienation. The creature is expelled from human society, longs for companionship and affection, and concludes that "I am malicious because I am miserable. Am I not shunned and hated by all mankind (sic)? . . . I will revenge my injuries; if I cannot inspire love."[36] The creature says that his misery is in his loneliness and his yearning for love. Since he is a creature with a body he longs for intimacy. He goes on to demand a female companion from his creator. "What I ask of you is reasonable and moderate; I demand a creature of another sex, but as hideous as myself: the gratification is small, but it is all that I can receive, and it shall content me."[37]

Victor Frankenstein also suffers alienation. Victor's isolation is self-imposed due to his inner demons, "secret toil," and self-deification. This mutuality in suffering is also the source of Frankenstein's denial and disinterest in the creature's interwoven destiny with him, its creator. The two are inseparable, and Shelley emphasizes this with the motif of the "double." Humans, created in God's image, have a profound capacity for ingenuity, compassion, and technological and scientific creativity. Yet humans must also live with the frightening reality of our dark side, shadow, or "double." Frankenstein refers to the creature as "my own spirit let loose from the grave forced to destroy all that was dear to me."[38] The civilized, compassionate, and respectable self is "shadowed" by the violent, egotistical, callous, repressed, and monstrous self. Our creations and their impact on the world reflect both these selves. This is why we must see their positive contributions and also their destructive capacities.

Human beings are interconnected with all things human and nonhuman. We are, therefore, subject to the consequences of our actions upon the same. The nonhuman creature is powerful and linked to its creator-antagonist. Therefore, Frankenstein is destined to share in its fate. Since we are deeply connected with the technologies we create, we must not subjugate our ethical considerations to our ambitions or ego. This is why careful consideration of new technologies is necessary (e.g., online bereavement and digital memorialization). We need to examine past human tendencies to

36. Shelley, *Frankenstein*, 131–32.
37. Shelley, *Frankenstein*, 133.
38. Shelley, *Frankenstein*, 64.

raise people above God, devalue the worth of created things, and downplay the human community, embodiment, and dependency on the incarnate and bodily resurrected Christ (e.g., Gnosticism).

Shelley reminds us that humans are intensely relational, interconnected, and fragile. But we also desire and experience the consequences of our scientific and technological creations. These creations can be expressions of our ambitions, egos, and god-complexes. Or they can be vehicles for healing, love, equality, dignity, and human flourishing.

CONCLUDING REFLECTION: GNOSTICISM, ONLINE BEREAVEMENT, AND DIGITAL MEMORIALIZATION

In the last two chapters, we have outlined the critical features of Christian Gnosticism of the second and third centuries. We have paid particular attention to gnostic perspectives on personhood, community, and engagement with the world and society. At the heart of Gnosticism is the conviction that spiritual things are good and material things are evil. Because matter is evil, the body is considered to be a tomblike prison. Both the body and the soul are corrupt and repulsive. The spirit is the only part of the human being that is redeemable.

Again, in the gnostic worldview, matter and bodies are evil. There is an overarching disdain for the created order and its worldly structures and an individualized approach to morality, social participation, and ethics. The gnostic dualistic worldview and its emphasis on individualized experience meant that its perspectives on community were a reaction against the existing church's institutionalism and other Hellenistic religious organizations and a manifestation of extremely individualized mythological perspectives. The gnostics' individualized and privatized spirituality matched their participatory, experiential, and decentralized understanding of community. Gnostic perspectives on community were never allowed to encroach on their privatized experience of the divine. Both the experiential and the privatized shaped their experience and expressions of human community.

Online bereavement and digital memorialization do not necessarily lead to gnostic inclinations toward hyperspirituality or their low views of creation, the body, and embodied human community. Yet without an understanding of Christian Gnosticism and its tendencies and beliefs, we (and mourners) may fall into some of the traps that the gnostics embraced. Those traps include views that elevate the spirit over the body, the metaphysical over the physical, and the disembodied soul over the community's embodied disciple. Caring professionals must understand how easy it is to slip into a disembodied view of the world, especially in a digital age. Online bereavement and digital memorialization are fine and may have an important place in grief, ritual, and memory for many. However, caring professionals must keep guiding people to healing, flourishing, and interpersonal connections that can only happen in the body and embodied community.

Michael Frost writes, "The term excarnation means to de-flesh, and is the opposite of the much more commonly used term, incarnation, which means to take on flesh."[39] He goes on to challenge Christians to pursue embodied, incarnational, and enfleshed faith and community.

> The trend toward excarnation has influenced the church and led to a disembodying of our faith . . . the excarnation of our theology, the exaltation of disengaged reason as the road to knowledge [which has culminated in] a disembodied approach to the mission of the church, a drift toward non-incarnational expressions, where disembodied advocacy is preferable to the dirt and worms and compost of localized service . . . I believe that in a time of disengagement and excarnation, the body of Christ is required all the more to embrace a more thoroughly embodied faith, a truly placed way of living that mirrors the incarnational lifestyle of Jesus. Now, more

---

39. Frost, "Christians, Engaged and Incarnate."

than ever, it seems, such a call to incarnational living needs to be heeded . . .[40]

As Frost concludes, "If I can glorify Christ in my body—whether by a fruitful life or by death—the body is a legitimate space, indeed, a sacred space . . . We are our bodies. We don't live in our bodies. And therefore our bodies and the bodies of others are precious and worthy of respect."[41]

---

40. Frost, *Incarnate*, 12.
41. Frost, *Incarnate*, 53.

5

Evaluating Therapeutic Responses to Bereavement Practices in the Digital Age

Early examples of online therapeutic responses include GriefNet (established in 1994), KIDSAID for grieving children (established in 1995), and personal or group blogs. We have also seen email networks (established in the 1980s), videoconferencing therapy, Skype- and Zoom-assisted therapy, grief and bereavement information websites, and online mourning and self-help groups. There is also the proliferation of interactive mourning communities that we observe today on SNSs and other platforms.[1]

During the early 2000s, Web 2.0 enabled users to communicate more interactively through sharing and collaboration of work and information on the internet without requiring web design or publishing skills.[2] Web 3.0, the latest in web applications, includes artificial intelligence in its design and application. Web 3.0 engages the dynamic content of Web 2.0 with enhanced efficacy in

---

1. Lynn and Rath, "Griefnet," 87–102.

2. Web 2.0 was first named by Darcy DiNucci in an article entitled "Fragmented Future" and popularized in 2004 by Tim O'Reilly and Medialive International: "What Is Web 2.0?" See Naik and Shivalingaiah, "Comparative Study."

machine interaction with devices such as mobile phones, home and office equipment, vehicles and appliances, and other equipment connected to the internet and digital platforms.[3] Information sharing moved from a "static" platform to a dynamic and interactive "smart" sharing environment. This move "socialized" content and contributed to the nascent digital death and grief mourning and therapeutic communities found today. These developments hold promise for future developments.

J. William Worden recognizes the emerging trend of SNSs and other online resources, named "cyber mourning" resources.[4] Worden identifies six current uses for these cyber mourning resources:

1. Online memorials.
2. Internet-based intervention.
3. Internet bereavement support groups.
4. Peer support web pages.
5. Psychoeducation.
6. Communicating with the deceased.

Private mourning experiences have moved to the public domain. Stillman discusses the complicated issue of Facebook as a medium for communication.[5] Some communicate their mourning experience as they would in person. For others, Facebook (and other SNSs) become a "social imaginary" where users may deviate from the private self. This approach to SNSs leads to a complex process of differentiation between private grief and online public mourning. This results in difficulty identifying true therapeutic needs on the one hand, and conversely, Facebook provides fertile space for new forms of meaningful interaction.

To evaluate existing therapeutic responses to loss and grief and death practices in the digital age context, one must consider

3. "Comparison between Web 2.0 and Web 3.0."
4. Worden, *Grief Counselling*, 1–3.
5. Stillman, "Virtual Graveyard," 46–47.

an overview of the most widely practiced counseling and therapeutic models and theories and reflect on how we can use them.

GRIEF WORK AND STAGE/PHASE MODELS

Leeat Granek, John James and Russell Friedman, and Tony Walter describe the twenty-first century as the period where grief became pathologized, medicalized, privatized, and professionalized.[6] Grief was traditionally regarded as part of everyday human life, experienced in the community, but became sequestered to private experience to be treated by professionals. Freud coined the term "grief work" in his 1917 "Mourning and Melancholia" and was one of the first to distinguish grief from depression. Freud believed people had to sever ties with the deceased for healthy resolution after loss. He worked towards a distinct ending point where mourners put the loss behind them and moved forward.[7] Grief work was deemed an emotional catharsis to release grief and included addressing each memory and expectation relating to the deceased. Melancholia would follow where the process failed. Grief work as the only model was later criticized as unhelpful to some as other theories and models developed.[8]

George Hagman describes the lack of empirical evidence found after studying Freud's "grief work" hypothesis over many years and highly criticizes the work as romanticized and standardized mourning, influenced by Victorian and Edwardian cultural beliefs about mourning.[9] Hagman's concern extended to the related mourning models that developed from Freud's work and even to the stage/phase models developed later that became the "new standard." He insists that we should acknowledge mourning

---

6. Granek, "Is Grief a Disease?," 264–77; James and Friedman, *Grief Recovery Handbook*, 3–17; Walter, "Different Countries"; Walter, "New Mourners"; Walter et al., "Die and Mourn."

7. Freud, "Mourning and Melancholia."

8. Doughty and Hoskins, "Death Education"; Fiorini et al., *On Freud's Mourning*, 4–7.

9. Hagman, *New Models*, i–xv, and 1–16.

and bereavement as a highly complex, unique, and individualized process experienced in a social context. We must incorporate intrapersonal, interpersonal, and intersubjective variables for every bereaved individual.

In the mid-1960s, stage models such as the Kubler-Ross model became the standard in treating grief. The Kubler-Ross model originally described the five grieving stages of terminally ill patients but was later applied to grief with the professional community's successful recognition. The five stages were denial, anger, bargaining, depression, and acceptance.[10] Other stage, phase, or task models grew in acceptance. These models became the standard in treating grief and bereavement. Elizabeth Doughty and fellow researchers, Kenneth Doka, Granek, James and Friedman, and Worden were concerned about the failure of these models to recognize the uniqueness and complexity of the individual grief experience, which professional carers may not appropriately address within a stage or phase-type model.[11]

Worden identifies four basic tasks that grieving individuals need to address in the cognitive process of grief:[12]

1. Accepting the reality of the loss.
2. Processing the pain of grief.
3. Adjusting to a world without the deceased.
4. Finding a way to remember the deceased whilst embarking on the rest of one's journey through life.

Although Worden identified four tasks, his later work increasingly regards the grieving process as fluid. He recommends seeing the tasks not as fixed processes or phases. Instead, people must revisit tasks multiple times, at various times, or at the same time.

10. Kübler-Ross, *On Death and Dying*, 51–146.
11. Doughty and Hoskins, "Death Education"; Doughty et al., "Current Trends"; Doka, "What's New in Grief?"; Granek, "Is Grief a Disease?"; James and Friedman, *Grief Recovery Handbook*; Worden, *Grief Counseling*.
12. Worden, *Grief Counseling*, 41–57.

Seemingly all four tasks can be accommodated within the digital or cyber mourning experience. But digital platforms must accommodate various mediators of mourning that may be individual to the mourner and expressed in a community or through individual posts and interactions. It is generally accepted that grieving is a social phenomenon. Grieving with others may instinctively and spontaneously emerge and prove significantly helpful to mourners.[13]

CONTINUING BONDS

During the twentieth century, one of the prevailing beliefs about a healthy grief resolution was the severing of ties with the deceased.[14] Contemporary research has shown that there has been much evidence supporting continuing bonds as a normal part of healthy adaptation. At the same time, there is evidence for maladaptive and detrimental consequences for continuing unhealthy bonds.

Digital platforms such as AfterTalk.com, developed by Lisa Bogatin and Larry Lynn in 2012, were designed to facilitate continuing bonds through grief support tools. These tools include writing and sharing with the deceased, close family, friends, or a therapist or caring professional.[15] The ongoing dialogue serves to alleviate the grief experience as mourners share their feelings, beliefs, joys, and frustrations with their deceased loved one.

Dennis Klass and Tony Walter recognize four areas of continuing bonds between the bereaved and deceased: (1) sensing the presence of the dead; (2) talking *to* the dead; (3) use of the

---

13. Giaxoglou et al., "Networked Emotions"; Granek, "Is Grief a Disease?," 267–76; Hutchings, "Death, Emotion"; Sofka et al., "Thanatechnology," 5–8; Stillman, "Virtual Graveyard," 50–58; Walter, "New Mourners"; Worden, *Grief Counseling*, 73.

14. Doughty and Hoskins, "Death Education"; Doughty et al., "Current Trends"; Freud, "Mourning and Melancholia," 243–58; Strobel, *Metamorpha*; Stroebe et al., "Attachment in Coping."

15. Bogatin and Lynn, "Aftertalk."

deceased as a moral guide (adoption or rejection of their value system); and (4) talking *about* the dead. All four areas apply to both the physical and digital worlds and are operational in both.[16]

Kathleen Gilbert and Michael Massimi describe the internet as a welcoming, large, and growing thanatechnology resource that enables mourners to maintain a connection with the deceased and fellow mourners and legitimizes both the mourner and the loss.[17] Ubiquitous or pervasive computing, especially with the universal use of "smart" mobile phone devices, enables users to "take" their deceased loved ones wherever they go and continue their bonds with the deceased ubiquitously.

Margaret Stroebe and her fellow researchers suggest that neither the long-standing beliefs of relinquishing bonds with the deceased nor the current focus on continuing bonds should be regarded as an either/or decision. Instead, the person coping with bereavement should be considered. Carers must also consider the process or "underlying dynamic" through which continuing or relinquishing bonds may be reached in adaptation.[18] They suggest evaluating relational theoretical considerations as bereavement relates to the ending of human relationships. They advise considering attachment theory as an excellent heuristic framework for understanding continuing bonds.

ATTACHMENT THEORY

We now consider attachment theory, the dual process model, constructivism, and adaptive grieving styles. Each of these is outlined helpfully in this order by Elizabeth A. Doughty, Adriana Wissel, and Cyndia Glorfield in "Current Trends in Grief Counseling." They list these four as "multiple theoretical orientations." We recommend you read the article.[19] They write:

16. Doughty and Hoskins, "Death Education"; Doughty et al., "Current Trends"; Klass and Walter, "Processes of Grieving."

17. Gilbert and Massimi, "From Digital Divide," 20–21.

18. Stroebe et al., "Continuing Bonds."

19. Doughty et al., "Current Trends," 4–7. In this chapter, we follow

Counselors need to be aware of the current trends in grief counseling, which include recognizing the uniqueness of the griever, questioning the grief work hypothesis, continuing bonds with the deceased, recognition of culture, and the use of multiple theoretical models that reflect these trends. It is critical that practicing counselors continue to consider new research and methods of conceptualizing individuals facing grief and loss in order to better meet the client's unique needs.[20]

So let's begin with attachment theory. Worden asserts that for one to grasp the "impact of loss and the human behavior associated with it, one must have an understanding of the meaning of attachment."[21] John Bowlby's attachment theory conceptualizes grief as separation anxiety resulting from the disruption of an attachment bond.[22] His theory asserts that parental attachment pattern in childhood determines one's reactions to loss later in life. Margaret Stroebe and colleagues integrated attachment theory after studying multiple theorists on attachment theory and further contemporary studies relating to the idea. They identified four different styles of attachment: (1) secure (showing the highest levels of psychological well-being after bereavement); (2) dismissing; (3) preoccupied; and (4) disorganized.[23]

Stroebe and company conclude that attachment styles influence the course, intensity, and manner of grieving after an attachment figure's death.[24] They caution against overgeneralizing grief according to attachment styles as types can be flexible. Though fairly consistent, types may change over time. They recommend further research, especially as it impacts bereavement.

Doughty, Wissel, and Glorfield's titles: attachment theory, the dual process model, constructivism, and adaptive grieving styles.

20. Doughty et al. "Current Trends," 7.
21. Worden, *Grief Counseling*, 15.
22. Bowlby, *Loss*, 138–69.
23. Stroebe et al., "Attachment in Coping," 56–59.
24. Stroebe et al., "Attachment in Coping."

Robert Neimeyer and Jason Holland assert that the perspective of the continuing bond extends attachment theory. This perspective develops new understandings of the relationship between mourner and deceased during the "aftermath of bereavement."[25] Digital platforms facilitate this development and extension through their pervasive use in connecting mourners to their deceased loved ones. These help mourners make sense of their loss. Such platforms help meet grief-related needs. Grief-related behaviors of mourners on these digital platforms can be accessed and assessed by researchers to observe and determine attachment-related adaptation after loss and bereavement. Websites and SNSs such as Facebook offer helpful education on attachment theory and bereavement and caring professionals offering their services.

DUAL PROCESS MODEL

Margaret Stroebe and Henk Schut consider the cautions and shortcomings of traditional theoretical models in bereavement, including grief work hypothesis, relinquishing and continuing bonds, and attachment theory. Out of this examination, they developed their framework for their dual process model (DPM).[26] The model integrates aspects of other models and theories and identifies two types of stressors:

1. Loss-oriented: related directly to the death and the feelings associated, such as focusing on the actual circumstances of death and emotions associated with the deceased.
2. Restoration-oriented: related to the secondary losses associated with the death, such as emerging new roles for the bereaved, fashioning a new life after the deceased has left, and new modes of relating to family and friends.

The DPM identifies a regulatory coping process of oscillation between attending to loss-oriented and restoration-oriented

---

25. Niemeyer and Holland, "Bereavement," 2.
26. Stroebe and Schut, "Dual Process Model."

stressors and periods where grief is not the focus. The model deems this process of oscillation *adaptive coping* and considers it a healthy response to loss. It also supports the need for respite from attending to either of the stressors as integral to adaptive coping.[27] Doughty and colleagues describe the DPM as unique in its consideration and encapsulation of other models to deliver a more comprehensive picture of grief.[28] This oscillation between stressors and periods of respite is evident in posts and interaction online in a digital context.

CONSTRUCTIVISM

Constructivism theorizes that humans construct meaning or reality through how they make sense of their experiences, perceptions, and narratives. Doughty and colleagues state that "constructivist thinking emphasizes multiple truths as organized by each individual."[29] Bereaved individuals are challenged to re-examine their world and to reconstruct new meaning without their loved one. Niemeyer and company reviewed several converging research programs and their results to conclude that meaning-making was a predictor of bereavement outcomes and serves as a moderator to reduce distress for mourners, often even to the point of nonsignificance.[30] Higher levels of meaning-making themes such as benefit-finding and positive identity change are linked with lower levels of bereavement complications. Evgenia Milman and colleagues found that specific meaning reconstruction themes played mediating roles in the development of prolonged grief disorder (PGD) following violent loss. This finding highlighted the potential benefits of a "meaning-based interventions approach" with these mourners. Milman and company discuss the growing recognition

---

27. Stroebe and Schut, "Dual Process Model."
28. Doughty et al., "Current Trends."
29. Doughty et al., "Current Trends," 5.
30. Niemeyer and Holland, "Bereavement."

of post-traumatic growth (PTG), where losing loved ones catalyzes positive bereavement outcomes.[31]

Laurie Burke and colleagues write about meaning reconstruction after loss and link faith, love, and loss in bereavement. They discuss the efficacy of various helpful interventions in meaning reconstruction. These include three interventions: (1) imaginal dialogues (therapist facilitating dialogues between bereaved and deceased, role-played by a mourner); (2) unsent letters to the deceased (reopening contact with deceased); and (3) life imprints (facilitated by a caring professional for a mourner to help them seek strands of continuity with the deceased. These include written letters, surveys, and direct telling).[32]

Burke and Neimeyer found that spirituality and religion help mourners adapt to bereavement and reconstruct meaning. Spirituality and religion may offer preinformed frameworks of understanding existentialist ideas and themes.[33] For some, religion provided guidance and understanding in reconstructing meaning and finding direction in life. For others, the study found bereavement might develop into a crisis of faith, testing their spiritual resilience and resources. This crisis can leave some feeling spiritually incapacitated or weary while grieving. Others may experience a vacillation between conviction of beliefs and doubt. Mourners experience spiritual processes that may differ from pre-loss faith and spiritual activities and might act as a panacea against faith crises. Burke and her colleagues recommend that helping professionals, including clergy, mental health workers, and other professionals, should "creatively facilitate psychological accommodation and spiritual progress" in mourners who experience spiritual difficulty in the process of making spiritual sense of their loss.[34] Suggested interventions include:

31. Milman et al., "Prolonged Grief Symptomatology."
32. Burke et al., "Faith, Love, and Loss," 13–20.
33. Burke and Neimeyer, "Spiritual Distress"; Burke et al., "Faith, Love, and Loss."
34. Burke et al., "Faith, Love, and Loss."

- Narrative therapy (written).
- Facilitating conversations between the deceased and God (verbal).
- Using Scripture to address concerns raised.
- Facilitating role-playing between a mourner and their faith community (friends and family).

Burke and Neimeyer found in their work with Christian mourners that when helping professionals implemented faith crisis interventions designed explicitly for spiritual sense-making, distressed mourners were virtually nonexistent.[35]

Caring professionals can easily facilitate written interventions and activities on online platforms in emails, blogs, and SNSs. These interventions are often incorporated into therapeutic practices. Written accounts and mourning activities are invariably visible in public memorialized or "live" sites as mourners communicate their ideas, feelings, meaning creation, and spiritual and religious beliefs (intentionally or inadvertently).

Korina Giaxoglou found that through Facebook, mourners have increased opportunity to create a sense of social support through narrative interactions. Facebook offers a means of entextualizing mourning in general.[36] Giaxoglou provides an analysis of mourning on Facebook through the process of entextualizing the content in three areas:

1. The death event.
2. Alignment or misalignment between the deceased and the network of mourners.
3. The poster's ideas, themes, and identity.

The study found that the networked posts on Facebook memorial sites organize narratives for meaning-making "out of the meaninglessness" of the death. Online memorial sites facilitate

---

35. Burke and Neimeyer, "Spiritual Distress."
36. Giaxoglou et al., "Networked Emotions."

storytelling of the painful experiences and make sense of networked mourners' ambient associations.

Birgit Wagner and Andreas Maercker developed a text and internet-based writing technique, *Interapy*, for bereaved adults suffering from trauma-related losses. This technique facilitated the mourner's expression and construction of a coherent narrative that may enable the integration of thoughts and feelings into the bereaved's lives.[37] *Interapy* practices consisted of self-confrontation, cognitive restructuring, and social sharing (email or Facebook). There have been several such internet-based programs with the advantages of anonymity and lack of geographical boundaries. These show promise as a new modality in bereavement therapy.

ADAPTIVE GRIEVING STYLES

Kenneth Doka and Terry Martin produced a model of adult grief that addresses individual mourners' unique and complex use of cognitive, behavioral, and affective strategies in adjusting to loss.[38] They identified diverse variables that affect an individual's grieving style, such as the culture, personality, experience, and gender, and identified three general "patterns." Patterns of grief are identified by the mourner's internal experience of loss and their external expression of grief, with grievers somewhere on a continuum. The patterns are:

1. Intuitive grieving—intense or heightened experience and expression of emotion coupled with the desire to communicate with others, in an attempt to work through their pain and adapt to their loss.

2. Instrumental grieving—cognitive, controlled approach to grieving with focus on practical tasks and problem solving. Emotions are managed rather than expressed and it is theorized that their emotional experience is less intense than

---

37. Wagner and Maercker, "Internet-Based Writing," 201–4.
38. Doka and Martin, *Grieving Beyond Gender*, ii–xiii.

intuitive mourners. They may view the grief experience as more of a challenge to master than a threat.

3. Blended grieving—most mourners employ a combination of both affective strategies (intuitive) and cognitive strategies (instrumental) and one strategy/style usually dominates. Neither style is preferred but is recognized as an individual's unique experience and expression of grief.

Problems in grieving develop when mourners attempt to employ an approach to grieving that is not their natural style, often due to expectations that their natural style is not acceptable or deemed inappropriate. The misalliance creates "dissonance," unsettles the natural grieving process, and may lead to complications.[39] Elizabeth Doughty and Wendy Hoskins warn that caring professionals should be careful not to "layer" their cultural expectations or preferred adaptations onto mourners. Carers must not assume that mourners fall within their dominant culture. Instead, carers must conceptualize and explore the mourner's culture, belief system, and natural grieving style.[40]

Doka and Martin, Stroebe and Schut, and Stroebe and company support the theory that gender affects grief and bereavement.[41] Women are generally more emotional in experience and expression. Men are usually more cognitive in their experience, avoiding emotional expression and experiencing more anger. Doughty and Hoskins argue that although gender may influence style, it does not determine it. Expectations regarding styles and gender roles may contribute to dissonance.[42] They further recommend that caring professionals conceptualize their clients from a sociocultural, globally sensitive, and intrapersonal perspective.

39. Doka and Martin, *Grieving Beyond Gender*.
40. Doughty and Hoskins, "Death Education."
41. Doka and Martin, *Grieving Beyond Gender*; Stroebe and Schut, "Dual Process Model"; Klass and Walter, "Processes of Grieving"; Stroebe et al., eds., *Handbook of Bereavement Research*.
42. Doughty and Hoskins, "Death Education."

CONTROVERSY

Research in grief and bereavement areas has shown significant variances in opinions regarding the different grief models and efficacy of theories. This variance results in the development of new models, the fusion of differing models, and the rejection of some. Doughty and colleagues and Kori Novak discuss recent controversies in grief counseling and compare various models and theories.[43] Both studies acknowledge the individuality of mourners. Doughty and Hoskins discuss the pitfalls of choosing only one therapeutic grief model that may suit some mourners but could adversely affect the grief outcomes of others. They recommend an individualized analysis of grief needs and the natural styles of mourners.[44] Novak agrees and suggests determining what models and interventions would best suit the needs of the individual mourner.[45]

The proliferation of online grief counseling support by caring professionals and organizations joins existing online grieving communities to provide counseling and peer support. These online grief counseling initiatives may help mourners find the best suited and supportive caring professional or grieving community. Finding this support may be problematic without the help of the internet.[46]

OTHER LESS WIDELY HELD THEORIES AND MODELS

Over the past two decades, various "new" theories, models, and frameworks have developed as helping professionals from multiple fields have analyzed existing theories and models. These caring professionals have contributed from their research and disciplines to existing bereavement knowledge. We briefly examine a few here.

43. Doughty et al., "Current Trends"; Novak, "Examination of Grief."
44. Doughty and Hoskins, "Death Education."
45. Novak, "Examination of Grief."
46. Gilbert and Massimi, "From Digital Divide," 21.

New Mourning Theory

Hagman developed a new mourning theory from various sources and not from any particular affiliations, schools, or theories. He used clinical observations made in daily practice by specialist psychoanalytically informed therapists, all of whom had similar findings.[47] The broad set of findings support counseling and pastoral practice informed by intrapersonal, interpersonal, and intersubjective experiences. This approach is an individualized process. Therapists provide bespoke solutions to mourners after carefully considering their unique and distinct grief experience and their internal and external mourning processes.

Task-Centered Approach

This approach is predominantly informed from a social work perspective, moving away from concentration on psychosocial casework towards shorter-term intervention methods. This approach focuses on the specific problems encountered and finds more individualized solutions suited to particular clients. Cultural influences and norms are carefully considered, especially those relating to death and bereavement. The focus becomes more solution-focused than problem-focused. Caring professionals and bereaved clients mutually agree on outcomes and objectives, and the client is the primary change agent. This approach is appropriate within culturally diverse communities and situations.[48]

The Grief Recovery Method

James and Friedman started their Grief Recovery Action Program in the mid-1980s. They gained recognition and a following in Canada and the United States. Their seminars and certification programs operated in many other Western countries, including

---

47. Hagman, *New Models*, i–xv and 1–16.
48. Drenth et al., "Complicated Grief."

Evaluating Therapeutic Responses to Bereavement Practices

Australia.[49] The program offers a series of "small and correct choices" and specific actions needed to move beyond loss. These include:

- choosing to recover.
- setting guidelines for recovery.
- identifying short-term energy relievers.
- preparing and working with a "loss history graph."
- "completing" losses (in all areas).
- completing and working with relationship graphs.
- other actions and choices.

Clients and therapists work together in decision-making processes and decide on targets and specific situations. Their approach includes most spheres of life: family, relationships, all losses, work, finance, and faith.

---

49. James and Friedman, *Grief Recovery Handbook*.

6

Constructing New Bereavement Practices in the Digital Age

Spontaneous mourning communities have emerged online over the past few decades in response to mourning individuals and needs of communities. The death of celebrities has led to the launch of many such communities as mourners endeavor to come to terms with the death of their celebrated heroes or role models, attempt to continue bonds with them, access new information, and collaborate in adding to or building new identities for the celebrated deceased. Mourners usually contribute their technospiritual views in online communication regarding the deceased's afterlife experience or destination. Mourners add technospiritual forms of encouragement and comfort to their fellow bereaved mourners and communicate with the deceased in the expectation that they receive their communication. Some even venture into meaning-making through constructing orientating beliefs and new narratives after the death-related loss.

A Facebook search uncovered an overabundance of public and private grief, mourning, and bereavement groups with thousands of members and often hundreds of thousands of "likes." Examples of such groups include Motherless Daughters, Christian Grief Survivors Group, Bereavement/Grieving Peer Support

Group, Professional Loss Grief Support Group, and the Suicide Support Group, to name a few. Most of these groups were created in the past ten years, many even more recently. All groups show daily activity with new posts by members ranging between eleven to 150 per day. Most of these groups were created by individuals due to their own grief experiences and are open to anyone with genuine grief experiences. These groups provide a safe place to share, vent, grieve, and receive encouragement and grief-related information.

Facebook facilitates multiple groups dedicated to bereavement therapy and counseling services for therapeutic and educational purposes. Much advertising of professional services takes place on SNSs such as Facebook. Bereavement counseling and therapy are no different. Therapeutic organizations and practices advertise and provide services such as introducing and facilitating support groups, face-to-screen counseling, educational videos, and infographic material. With the advent of the COVID-19 pandemic at the start of 2020, therapeutic professionals were restricted from practicing person-to-person and moved counseling, pastoral, and spiritual care practice to digital platforms such as Facebook, YouTube, Zoom, WhatsApp (video), Facebook Messenger (video), Skype, Google Hangout, and more. Digital platforms provide non-geographical and nonmaterial locations for counseling and educational services that can be recorded (with consent), watched multiple times, stored safely electronically, and enable functioning of support groups. Digital platforms and technologies are simple to initiate and maintain. Where access and technical knowledge are problematic for clients, telephone conversations are easy substitutes. They have been used for decades when physical distance impedes therapeutic access and practice. Increased digital delivery of professional services should continue beyond the COVID-19 restrictions as mechanisms have been implemented and will continue to reduce caring professional-client barriers.

Several Facebook bereavement support groups spontaneously initiated online group "chats" through online videoconferencing platforms for the first time. Mourners were searching for community since they were restricted from social interaction during the internationally applied COVID-19 restrictions. Membership of private "chat groups" on Facebook increased. These "chats" are expected to continue or even lead to formal gatherings in the future, as evidenced in the comments sections of these groups. Numerous posts were made from March to April 2020, expressing increased grief experiences due to the isolation.[1] Posts such as "This epidemic makes my grief experience worse . . . ugg 😩," "lockdown is getting to me," "my grandma died today, because of this stupid COVID19 we couldn't be with her in hospital . . . COVID tied my hands," "coronavirus and still grieving . . . so sad and angry!!!," "thank you for this group . . . obviously existed before isolation but is clearly more important now than ever." These trends confirm Walter and Gilbert's view that mourners require community for support and connection. Mourners are either creating new or reaching out to existing mourning communities, searching for engagement and the healing narratives of fellow mourners.[2] Facebook as thanatechnology effortlessly supplies a platform that meets general mourning needs of memorialization, continuing bonds, meaning-making, technospirituality, community, identity formation and maintenance, and therapeutic and educational needs. This thanatechnology offers online validation of mourners' own grief experiences and helps people share within a mourning community about a particular death event. Such online technology allows mourners to reconstruct the identity of the deceased through their networks and online communities.[3]

During the early phases of the COVID-19 pandemic, membership numbers on Facebook bereavement groups increased. These numbers are not likely to decrease after "joining" and being added by administrators. New members introduce themselves, providing a narrative around their experience and reasons for joining. Existing members that are mental health professionals—such

---

1. Due to privacy laws and privacy settings within private groups, accurate references may not be cited.
2. Walter, "New Mourners"; Gilbert, "Death, Grief," 295–97.
3. Stillman, "Virtual Graveyard," 50.

Constructing New Bereavement Practices in the Digital Age

as caring professionals, mental health nurses, psychologists, and psychiatrists—are posting encouraging messages and offering free professional services. Various free summits and seminars for helping professionals have launched during this period with the expectation for more to follow. Many schools, universities, church organizations, individual churches, mental health organizations, and government bodies have launched online COVID-19 helping resources, chat groups, support groups, digital messages of encouragement, and information. The technology and platforms for further development and expansion of services remain. These platforms will improve and be used henceforth.

Due to social distancing restrictions during the COVID-19 pandemic, digital solutions have been initiated in some cases and continued in others for funerals and memorial services. These include live streaming, digital video messages from close family and friends, viewing of the deceased, and increased mobile phone video interaction with dying individuals. Increasingly, final goodbyes are being said through mobile phone video connections and applications. "Drive-in funeral theater" is being introduced where mourners pay tribute to their loved ones in the privacy and safety of their vehicles while watching the funeral.[4] Most funerals are being arranged online during this pandemic. Jasenka Jones concluded that online trade in the funeral industry is a growing interest commercially in Ireland and that cultural changes should ensue.[5] These findings are evidenced worldwide during the pandemic. Cultural norms and practices around death and dying are expected to continue to shift and evolve towards an increased acceptance of digital practice.

Facebook private groups for funeral practitioners have also emerged during this time, with groups such as "Funeral Practitioners COVID 19 Conversation," created on March 23, 2020, with 389 members and two new posts per day. Another group is the "Funeral Professionals Corona Discussion Page," created on March 17, 2020, with 124 members and two new posts per day to

---

4. Fowler, "Drive-in Funeral Theater."
5. Jones, "Towards an Understanding."

"share best practice around dealing with the coronavirus."[6] These newly formed groups, together with numerous existing groups, show interest around providing best practice during shifts in the funeral industry during the pandemic. Such changes are legal, commercial, and therapeutic in nature.

Michelle Aciavatti warns that denying proper comforting gathering rituals around death and dying is denying people their basic needs as humans of mediating their grief through the final farewell of a loved one.[7] The funeral industry, including practitioners such as funeral directors, clergy, chaplains, and celebrants, can provide a new way forward in providing mitigated rituals that continue to comfort and provide necessary community through the nascent thanatechnologies available. These new emerging technologies are here to stay and will continue to produce innovative solutions to the practices of death, dying, and bereavement.

Noe Kasali and a caring team of professionals developed effective alternative death and burial rituals in the Democratic Republic of the Congo (DRC) in 2018 after the Ebola epidemic. The lack of the deceased's body for burial caused severe disruption in cultural death and grieving rituals. The reinterpreted alternative rituals consisted of three steps facilitated by the caring professionals:

1. Gathering of loved ones at a chosen place of significance and asking questions regarding the death to replace a gathering with the newly cleansed and dressed body of the deceased.

2. Gathering to share memories through stories, photographs, song, and dance, to replace dancing and singing rituals at traditional funerals. Letters were also written to the deceased and kept in a designated place to reread later, replacing final farewells at funerals.

---

6. Parent Loss Grief Support Group, Facebook, January 12, 2017; Professionals Grief and Loss Network, Facebook, April 29, 2018; Funeral Professionals Corona Discussion Page, Facebook, March 17, 2020; Funeral Practitioners COVID 19 Conversation, Facebook, March 23, 2020.

7. Acciavatti, "Guest Post."

3. Planting trees or plants at designated places as living memorials to the deceased.[8]

This process of reinterpretation of clearly understood mourner needs in a particular cultural context is a powerful example of how needs can be met in unique or changing circumstances and then transformed and adapted to change or replace traditional rituals and practices. It is possible to convert or transform physical practices and rituals around death, dying, and bereavement. Existing emerging technologies or innovative new technologies can be a great asset in the digital age. Using Kasali's scenario, the transformation to digital practices could include a range of technologies consisting of online gatherings in digital spaces such as Facebook memorial or live pages where questions are asked and answered in video or written mode. These Facebook pages allow sharing songs, memories, photographs, and stories—these become bereavement and healing narratives. "Letters" or written memorials (posts) are effortlessly uploaded for continued meaning-making attempts in the healing process after death losses. These memorial pages or digital links to other memorialized pages can serve as digital memorials to the deceased. Mourners can revisit these memorials as often as they need or want to. Bonds with the deceased may be continued.

The emerging digital platforms offer obvious advantages and benefits for death and bereavement. However, it would be remiss to exclude a discussion of the potential for malaise and anguish for the bereaved due to unexpected or even unwelcome reminders of the deceased as "digital ghosts." Bjorn Nansen and colleagues refer to the restless dead in digital cemeteries that materialize on digital platforms and are "exhumed" in the technical connectivity of SNSs and other platforms.[9]

---

8. Gercama and Jones, "Alternative Mourning Rituals."
9. Nansen et al., "Restless Dead," 111.

UNEXPECTED AND UNWELCOME DIGITAL REMINDERS OF THE DEAD

Giaxoglou and company compare various studies in developed nations and conclude that the complexity and the dynamics of networked emotions and sharing publicly in loss-related contexts sometimes leads to discomfort and resistance. This happens due to divergent views of appropriateness and sensitivities of emotional sharing and boundaries. There can be confusion or disagreement around boundaries relating to life versus death expressions and biases in religious and cultural contexts (even within cultures).[10]

Walter states that online social media commemorations can "resemble a conflict-ridden cemetery."[11] These commemorations connect individuals that may never choose to associate outside the death-related context. Walter presents a few areas with potential difficulty for consideration:

- There is emerging social pressure to mourn deaths regardless of personal attachment, creating norms that mourners may find inappropriate.
- There is the problem of addressing the dead directly in interactions on Facebook.
- Technospirituality on Facebook can cause difficulties, where both religious and nonreligious post overtly Christian references to the afterlife such as heaven, angels, God, and more. Such posts can disturb secular mourners or mourners that knew the deceased as secular.

Other areas highlighted include:

- References to the afterlife that may be different from held beliefs and expectations.
- Language that assumes the dead have agency through their expectations that the deceased are receiving their communications.

10. Giaxoglou et al., "Networked Emotions."
11. Walter, "New Mourners."

Constructing New Bereavement Practices in the Digital Age

- Opposing views and opinions about the death event (suicide, accident, or overdose).

- The presence of "mourning trolls" (morbidly curious strangers who post faux condolences, jokes, or cruel comments or attack online mourning norms and cause distress to mourners who had close relationships with the deceased).

- Family members who are grieving may feel distraught by the frivolity, superficiality, and upbeat posts of younger individuals or well-wishers, some who only knew the deceased by association.

Brubaker and colleagues describe Facebook memorialized profiles as "interactive digital tombstones." The deceased, of course, cannot have a say about content. This can lead to conflicting narratives about the deceased, death event, and other mourners' authenticity. Conflict can emerge over the management and ownership of the profiles after death.[12] The broad social interaction promoted through Facebook and other SNSs may eliminate agency over how, why, and when mourners grieve. Late or accidental discoveries of deaths through Facebook posts can exacerbate this experience.

Many automated Facebook processes may trigger memories of deceased loved ones that serve as painful reminders for some. These include the following: (1) reminders of events and pictures posted at periods past (one, two, or five years ago); (2) most "liked" posts or pictures; (3) prompts to connect with "friends of friends"; (4) "suggested groups"; (5) "people you may know" picked up through email addresses or other contact information; and (6) general posts "liked" and comments by others. These digital ghosts persist and, for some, intensify and prolong their already intense grief experiences.

Hutching cautions that Facebook online bereavement groups that promise support have their own online emotional regimes and norms and may intensify the "sequestration of socially-problematic

---

12. Brubaker et al., "Beyond the Grave."

grief experiences."[13] This can happen through the gathering of the bereaved in private online groups away from public view and scrutiny.

Dark tourism or thanatourism is how death or tragedy sites are transformed into vicarious trauma vehicles, morbid curiosity, and popular tourist attractions.[14] Although only named in 1996, it has been well-established, commercialized, and commoditized for decades. Erin Dermody refers to it as the "Disneyfication" of tragedy. Facebook, voyeuristic in its architecture, effortlessly facilitates the curious and often ill-intentioned online visitors that "troll" memorialized spaces and produce anguish and suffering for the bereaved. According to Michael Arntfield, this "cheapens" the tributes and expressions of grief, memorialization, and connection between mourners and their deceased loved ones.

Defriending a deceased loved one's live or memorialized Facebook page remains an option for the bereaved. For the bereaved experiencing intense distress, this may afford an easy decision to end the torment of digital ghosts and unwelcome reminders. For many, the decision may never come. Some might delay that decision until they sense the decision would bring their bereavement journey to a healthy conclusion, and they would benefit from its permanence. The finality of such a farewell, forever foreclosing on the access to the "profile-turned-shrine," brings a bereaved person to the point of finality and permanence in their closure. Such closure may be similar to the "closure characteristics of traditional pre-Facebook times."[15]

---

13. Hutchings, "Death, Emotion," 200.
14. Dermody, "Dark Tourism"; Arntfield, "Ememoriam," 102–3.
15. Stillman, "Virtual Graveyard," 57.

7

Proposals for Bereavement Counseling and Pastoral and Spiritual Care in a Digital Age

We have offered a literary and theoretical exploration of the emerging phenomenon of the online interactions between the bereaved and the online presence of their bereaved loved ones. We have also evaluated existing therapeutic responses to loss, grief, and death practices in the online context. There are no "one-size-fits-all" approaches for counseling, pastoral, and spiritual care practitioners. Every mourner has their own individualized grief experience that relates to their attachment styles. This relates to their relationship with the deceased, desire or need for continuing bonds with the deceased, vacillating experience between expressing emotions relating to grief and problem solving, ideas regarding meaning-making and finding resolution, and other cultural, gender, and individualized contributing factors.

Research has provided evidence for newer concepts in bereavement and loss and grief counseling. These include:

1. Continuing bonds with the deceased instead of closure and "moving on."

2. Blended grieving styles.
3. Adaptive styles of grieving.
4. Individualized processes.
5. Vacillation of cognitive processing and experiences on a continuum.
6. Brief solution therapies.
7. Cognitive behavioral therapies around grief and loss.
8. Communal grieving.
9. Support groups.
10. Online therapies.
11. Narrative therapies.
12. Increased spirituality and technospirituality.

Ethically, caring professionals are and should be bound to the professional counseling or practitioner association or governing body that applies to their practice. Caring professionals are bound to certain fundamental ethical principles. These principles apply to both traditional counseling and pastoral and spiritual care, and to digital or internet-based counseling and pastoral and spiritual care. These include:

1. Autonomy of client: choice in counseling and pastoral and spiritual care, and negotiating the working relationship in digital counseling and pastoral and spiritual care.
2. Beneficence: the client's welfare and a good outcome is the priority.
3. Non-maleficence: avoiding any harm to the client through misuse or mishandling.
4. Justice: treating the client fairly.
5. Fidelity: keeping trust and good faith by honoring the professional integrity of the client-caring professional relationship.

Associations and regulatory bodies include the above principles and expand on these to include the following:

1. Maintenance and improvement of competency in professional standards in education and practice.
2. Commitment to ongoing personal and professional development.
3. Continued knowledge of theories and making suitable referrals where competent service cannot be provided.

These ethical considerations for caring professionals apply to all areas of counseling and pastoral and spiritual care, including grief, loss, and bereavement.

There are various advantages to online and digital counseling and pastoral and spiritual care. Convenience and the lack of geographical boundaries seem to be the most valued benefits. Other advantages include:

1. Finding choice providers in a client's cultural context and preferred language.
2. The empowerment of regionally located clients.
3. Counseling and pastoral and spiritual care for homebound clients (for example, the disabled, ill, or homebound due to culture, shame, or social stigma).
4. The online disinhibition effect, which leads to higher degrees of intimate self-disclosure.
5. The recording and printing of a conversation transcript with appropriate software capabilities (with consent).
6. The therapeutic effects of writing (typing) out considered responses in asynchronous counseling (delayed responses such as email exchanges).
7. The economic benefits of reduced costs of physical practice overheads.

8. Reduced educational material costs, as resources can be distributed through hyperlinks.[1]

The most mentioned disadvantage of online counseling and pastoral and spiritual care is that nonverbal clues and nuances are difficult to detect. There remains much debate about this issue. Training, increased attention to detail, asking specific and relevant questions, and increased experience may mitigate the perceived difficulties. Technological issues such as connectivity, skills deficiency, malfunctions, and software limitations are disadvantages that also hold mitigating factors such as training, increased technical skills and experience, and investment into superior digital technologies. Digital counseling and pastoral and spiritual care are expected to become more ubiquitous. Therefore, investments in education and training and paying attention to all mitigating factors should become a priority.

UNIQUENESS OF MOURNERS

Caring professionals should be curious about every individual mourner's experience and needs, offering tentative explorations such as those that follow: "What do you miss the most about your relationship?" "Tell me about the relationship with your family of origin, your mother or father." "Tell me more about what you feel that is missing." "I am curious about what you think grief should look like and how your experience is different." "Let us talk more about your previous losses and how you managed to journey through them." For the more spiritual or religious mourners, questions like these can be asked: "Where do you see God in this experience?" "How would you feel about writing to God about your thoughts and experience?" "Ask God any questions you may have." "What does Scripture say about God in your grief and experience of loss?"

Sincere curiosity expressed in tentative language with a strong therapeutic alliance with a client would help get to the root

1. Gamino, "Ethical Considerations."

of the bereaved's experience, needs, conflicts, ambivalences, and fears. Every mourner is a unique individual with unique experiences and cultural and environmental interpretations. These need to be understood and explored with the mourner without any preconceived ideas by the caring professional. Caring professionals are professional helpers that can tap into their skill set, education, intuition, and curiosity to develop a customized or bespoke therapeutic plan. Such helpers can then take evidence-based bereavement models and intuitive application thereof to a client after interpreting and understanding their needs. Such carers can then formulate counseling and pastoral and spiritual care plans that are flexible enough to accommodate new information or developments yet sound in theory and application.

INFORMED PRACTICE AND EDUCATION

Caring professional education considers the need for adaptation and change as counseling inherently fosters and facilitates change and empowerment for clients and patients. Caring professionals work with individuals who share human experiences, including loss, grief, and bereavement. Education and updated training in this field are vital in providing help during times of loss and bereavement. Much research in this area recommends continuous training for counseling, pastoral, and spiritual care practitioners nationally and internationally. This training can happen through professional development courses, formal education, seminars and webinars, keeping updated through academic and research journals, conferences, professional organizations, and accreditation standards. Training helps enhance professional practice, ensures the development of culturally informed practice, upholds the profession as a whole, and ensures client safety and well-being.

Digital proficiency and education in the digital age are essential for counseling, pastoral, and spiritual care practitioners. As discussed previously, mourners are increasingly becoming immersed in the digital bereavement world through online interaction in communities, SNS platforms such as Facebook on memorialized pages, live pages of the deceased, and private and public support groups and discussions. Online platforms meet needs previously ignored, and mourners spontaneously start new movements and communities as needs and opportunities emerge. Practitioners who are not developing professionally in the digital context will be "left behind" in developing trends, professional practice, business development opportunities, revenue generation, implementation of therapeutic interventions, and integrating strategies and new opportunities. Such opportunities include developing new online techniques, bereavement rituals and collaboration, or merging physical and digital practice interventions. Training and upskilling during crises and sudden change such as the COVID-19 pandemic will leave untrained practitioners lagging behind their peers and the industry. SNSs such as Facebook present lucrative business opportunities, effective platforms for training through online live or recorded Facebook summits, seminars and webinars, conferences, training modules, and professional development for caring professionals. SNSs may facilitate effective strategies for remaining informed of current professional practice norms.

Engaging the services of online business development organizations may help where such needs are assessed. Carers can enroll in digital training courses, seminars, summits, and conferences to help with training in the areas of online therapeutic practice in bereavement and loss, understanding digital technologies and their application, death studies (thanatology, thanatechnology, thanaspirituality, and ritual) in a digital context, business development and marketing, and ethical considerations in the digital world.

REINTERPRETING MOURNER NEEDS WITHIN THE DIGITAL CONTEXT

Well-trained caring professionals with a good understanding of grief, loss, and bereavement theory, models, and practice should be skilled to reinterpret individualized needs of the bereaved within a digital context. Mourner needs for memorialization can be expressed in a physical context by visiting burial grounds or ashes in an urn displayed in a home. Mourners can reinterpret these items in the digital context, whereby memorialized Facebook pages may be set up with digital images for the deceased to serve as a memorialized location for visitation. The need for open expressions of grief in a safe space can be reinterpreted in the digital context where a mourner joins a private Facebook bereavement group with similar circumstances (for example, suicide or parent groups). This reinterpretation process and associated benefits, where and if appropriate for a client, depending on their ideology towards the digital world and online social interaction, can be carefully explained. In collaboration, multiple suitable possibilities are available or can be created.

PROFESSIONAL REGISTRATION OF CARING PROFESSIONALS AND PASTORAL AND SPIRITUAL CARERS

The same basic ethical principles that govern traditional counseling should be adhered to in digital counseling and pastoral and spiritual care. These adherences might be the same in principle but could be presented differently, for example, in automated digital contracts, referrals, and education. Regulatory standards and requirements should be extended in a digital context to include considerations such as privacy laws and associated issues, relevant advertising and marketing laws, registration and maintenance of internet domains, digital storage solutions and laws, maintenance and ownership of digital content, contractual agreements, and associated laws and regulations relating to digital content and copyright laws.

Professional supervision is required for caring professionals by associations and professional bodies and extends to include pastoral supervision of caring professionals and pastoral carers. Supervision depends on the governing body and usually requires a predetermined ratio of supervision hours to counseling and pastoral and spiritual care hours. Supervision ensures compliance with the relevant legal, ethical, and professional practice standards and is focused on the caring professional and their competence, training, welfare, conduct, business practice and development, and other issues that may arise.

DEVELOPING HEALTHY DIGITAL BOUNDARIES FOR CLIENTS

For clients that would benefit from digital interaction or are already interacting spontaneously, considerations should include setting up healthy digital boundaries. Anecdotal evidence shows that during the COVID-19 pandemic, individuals are being overwhelmed by overexposure to media content. Healthy boundaries could be discussed and developed collaboratively and may include the following: (1) maximum hours per day on Facebook and other digital platforms relating to bereavement, grief, and loss; (2) how often a client should or may check status updates on memorialized and live pages of the deceased or support groups; (3) disabling notifications on Facebook in general or specific pages, friends, or groups; (4) decisions and discussions with the appropriate people and organizations regarding maintenance or ownership of a memorialized page; (5) considering the digital legacy of the deceased: if relevant discovering its financial value, copyright issues, intellectual property rights, and distribution of digital "items"; and (6) discussing potentially distressing issues found online with a client. These issues may include inappropriate emotional responses of others, differing narratives regarding persons or events, trolls, dark tourism, finding previously unknown information about the deceased, and more.

DIGITAL TECHNOLOGIES

Caring professionals should be aware of relevant digital technologies and thanatechnology and be trained in their relevant choices. The principle of "simplest is best" may apply to most clients, especially older groups, but a knowledgeable and sensitive discussion with clients, considering their needs and discoveries, is best. For some clients using FaceTime on their Apple device is most sensible for a counseling session, while a Zoom session makes more sense for others. Some might use more complex digital imaging software to create content for memorialized pages. Others might comment on a Facebook page.

Navigating online platforms such as Facebook should be considered by caring professionals in following bereavement trends, marketing their practice, watching online content for training, education, and professional development, and connecting with other practitioners in professional networking groups. Using platforms to deliver best practice should include training in platforms such as Skype, Zoom, Google Hangout, and more.

Training in automated digital processes should be considered for counseling, pastoral, and spiritual care practices. Such digital tools include automated generation of counseling contracts, calendar syncing, and sending reminders and confirmations to clients regarding appointments. Other online electronic tools include generating invoices and receipts, questionnaires, feedback forms, supervision contracts and appointments, training reminders, booking and offering professional development, presenting digital content, and automated digital file storage. The benefits include maintaining high professionalism and efficiency standards and ensuring that essential processes are not missed and are time efficient.

Digital platforms and web development, in general, are still in their infancy. Considering the speed of their evolution and development over the past decade, modes of digital remembrance, providing therapeutic help to mourners, and delivering online content, education, and training will continue to undergo transformations and transmutations before expectations regarding a sense of permanence are reached. Therefore, a continued sense of learning, discovery, innovation, networking, and training is proposed for caring professionals, thana-educators, and death practitioners such as funeral practitioners, celebrants, and clergy.

The Soul Online

Digital innovations for death and dying practice and ritual could include the following types of things: (1) "speaking from the grave"—recorded messages prepared before death to be released online at funerals or memorials, anniversaries, and special occasions; (2) recording messages, writing digital letters, releasing digital images such as photos, videos, and songs, and producing digital memorialized "packages" to be distributed online (and physically) after a person's death; and (3) the use of artificial intelligence (AI).

Artificial intelligence can be used to develop applications where mourners can ask advice from their "deceased loved ones" through a hologram-type application or more static impressions after much input, including interviews, surveys from family and friends, voice recordings, photos and images, and journals. These may reproduce gathered information in the deceased's voice with images displayed of the deceased. AI and robotics developments could also lead to the development of digital replicas of the deceased loved ones (voice, image, ideas, views, beliefs, and values) on digital platforms or through other robotic developments. AI and 3D technologies combined can create a 3D-type funeral, memorial, and gravesite experiences or a visit with the deceased loved one. Digital cemeteries and memorialized symbolic items such as digital candles, digital bouquets, and digital tombstones have existed for decades but remain open for further development and innovation. The development of automated responses from the deceased to the mourners as they post in memorialized Facebook pages, generated after significant data inputs and sophisticated word recognition technologies (used already by large corporations and government bodies in their online help forums), is another possibility.

SUPPORT GROUPS

Support groups vary in terms of structure, availability, function, and who facilitates or leads them. There are peer-led, self-led, and professional-led support groups. They are also private (accepted members only see contributions) or public (anyone sees all

Bereavement Counseling and Pastoral and Spiritual Care in a Digital Age

information) in a digital context. There is a recent development in Japan with an emerging professional called a "self-help supporter," for whom the functioning of the group dynamic supersedes the individual's functioning. This may present new opportunities for caring professionals who decide to develop their understanding and skills in this area and practice accordingly. The functioning of support groups is easily transferrable to a digital setting. This is one of many such developments and opportunities, and caring professionals should be aware of developments in group work and be prepared to innovate where appropriate.

INNOVATION FOR COUNSELING AND PASTORAL AND SPIRITUAL CARE PRACTICE

Caring professionals should use their intuitive thinking and curiosity to innovate. Innovation is already seen in theories and models applied in fresh ways suited for individual clients. For digital practice, those innovations can easily be adapted and adjusted to fit platforms and needs. Joining counseling and therapy forums is recommended, specifically in bereavement and in other areas in counseling and pastoral and spiritual care where techniques or interventions can be adapted for grief, loss, and bereavement. Innovations from bereavement theories and models could include recordings and video clips made by a caring professional for clients regarding "what to expect" from bereavement, an explanation of particular theories or models, "myths about bereavement," suggestions for emotional regulation, explanation of interventions such as narrative exercises, and "homework" recordings made by caring professionals or clients. These can be posted on platforms privately, publicly, to support groups, during counseling and pastoral and spiritual care sessions, to peer groups, and more. Other innovations could include education technologies, such as interactive training and education on digital platforms and video or interactive training, webinars, summits, and supervisors' conferences. (Education can include training caring professionals about supervision, training new supervisors, providing professional development in this area, and peer-to-peer supervision training.) Videos can be sent to clients or watched while in an online counseling session regarding "generic" issues such as caring professional-client boundaries, confidentiality, agreements, and handling crises. Online training can be produced in video format, recorded or live, for creative interventions around creating digital (or physical) collages of the lives and memories of the deceased, art or expression therapies (arts, music and drama), role plays, and more. There are also mentoring opportunities where digital natives (digital generations) can mentor digital immigrants (new to the digital world) regarding technologies in a digital bereavement context.

The digital world is one of innovation. Every upgrade, new version, new software, or web-enabling development—and development in other technologies such as robotics, AI, and electronics—produces more opportunity for adaptation, add-on services, and innovation. The endless possibilities are ever-increasing, with no limits to future innovation. The impacts and consequences for mourners and the bereaved create increased responsibility for regulators, caring professionals, death practitioners, and thanaeducators to remain within legal, regulatory, and ethical boundaries and norms.

8

Recommendations for Further Research and Study

Various researchers recommend additional or increasing education and further research into up-to-date education for caring professionals and practitioners in the area of loss, grief, bereavement, death, and dying.[1] This would extend to education and research in the same areas of counseling and pastoral and spiritual care in an ever-increasing digital context with its unique implications, applications, and reach.

Increasing interest in spirituality and religion and its effects on the bereaved in a digital age requires further research. These effects include crisis-of-faith, meaning-making, healthy resolution, effects on risk factors for complicated grief, and effects in different cultures, genders, and individualized circumstances.[2]

Research into bereavement in a digital context on social media platforms (Facebook, Instagram, and Twitter) has produced evidence for the phenomenon of technospirituality.

1. Gamino, "Ethical Considerations"; Sofka et al., "Thanatechnology"; Sofka, "Net Generation"; Doughty and Hoskins, "Death Education"; Doughty et al., "Current Trends,"; Burke et al., "Faith, Love, and Loss."

2. Burke et al., "Faith, Love, and Loss"; Milman et al., "Prolonged Grief Symptomatology"; Neimeyer et al., "Continuing Bonds."

Technospirituality includes overtly spiritual and religious references regarding death, dying, bereavement, and overtly Christian references to the afterlife in digital and social networking spaces. All forms, effects, and aspects of technospirituality, and spirituality and religious themes in a digital context, require further research and study.[3] We recommend research into the digital afterlife. Does what is written change the held beliefs of writers or readers? Do their personal beliefs hold in digital communications? Are they holding separate afterlife belief systems? What is the impact of overtly Christian digital afterlife communication on readers of other religions? Do these Christian afterlife communications extend to Christian eschatological ideas?

We recommend investigations into general, specific, and newly designed spiritual and religious assessments and interventions for relieving psychospiritual distress, applied online for bereaved clients, support groups, and training and education to caring professionals.

"Netiquette" is a word gaining recognition and refers to etiquette as users interact online: their language, expectations and appropriateness of interaction, appropriate "manners," and entextualizing. Mourners are sometimes distraught by some users' lack of netiquette or their lack of understanding in context. Online communication relies mainly on language and text interpretation with the general absence of facial expression, body language, voice volume, and any knowledge of the individual communicating. Exploration into netiquette and its lack of governance, impact, and consequences on the bereaved should be considered.

We recommend research into "internet counseling and pastoral and spiritual care" as a modality. Internet counseling and pastoral and spiritual care require a unique skill set, including the following: technology skills; innovative, creative, and flexible application of known modalities and theories; intuitive reinterpretation of mourner needs in a digital context; electronic boundaries

---

3. Milman et al., "Prolonged Grief Symptomatology"; Brubaker and Vertesi, "Death and the Social Network"; Brubaker and Hayes, "We Will Never Forget"; Walter, "New Mourners"; Castro and Gonzales, "Afterlife Presence."

Recommendations for Further Research and Study

(absence of personal presence, body language interpretation, absence of smell, and more); electronic fluidity (physical and digital merging, geographical mobility, and multiple applications) and a heightened sense of ethics among helping professionals.

We recommend further investigation into five crucial areas: (1) both caring professionals' and clients' perceptions of internet counseling, as these views emerge from culture, gender, mental health issues, and comfortable internet users versus rare or nonusers; (2) exploration into "normal grievers" versus grievers with complications such as complicated grief, disenfranchised grief, anticipatory grief, delayed grief, and more; (3) the consideration of different bereavement theories and models applied online and their benefits, limitations, effects, and outcomes; (4) further assessment into the influence of internet counseling and pastoral and spiritual care on the therapeutic alliance between caring professionals and clients; and (5) additional enquiry into internet counseling for mourners during times of crises (including suicide and self-harm).

Caring professionals are accustomed to assessing clients for risk of suicide, self-harm, domestic and family violence, complicated grief, and more. Internet counseling presents a unique problem concerning the accuracy of risk assessment. Caring professionals also assess the proximity of clients to crisis help services, such as hospitals, and the accessibility of services, such as access to paramedics and police. Contact details of a client should be made easily accessible, (alternative) phone device nearby to contact services, and an allowance given for the time to stay "with" a client. Reliability of connection and an established therapeutic alliance are also important. Research into all aspects of clients at risk and counseling bereaved clients (and others) is recommended. Additional studies into the efficacy of online interventions for bereaved clients during crises and their efficacy are highly recommended.

Further examination of the bereaved's overattachment to the deceased loved one's online presence is necessary. This is both in terms of strong connections (close family and friends) and weaker connections (friends of friends and acquaintances), particularly on dynamic sites such as Facebook.

Exploration into responsible management, ownership, copyright, intellectual property rights, distribution of digital assets, guardianship, and privacy issues regarding the deceased's continuing online presence on Facebook is advised in all its facets and areas of reach.

Continued investigation of the efficacy of newly created digital death, grief, and loss rituals for mourners' improved outcomes is recommended. Does the continued digital, interactive, and dynamic social presence and restless posthumous existence of the deceased loved one benefit the mourner longer term? Does the online support group for the bereaved replace or support present needs for community or detract from healthy social functioning in the community? Are smart devices and their portability—that facilitate increased interaction with the deceased's online presence—improving or reducing healthy adaptation after bereavement? Addressing the dead directly on social platforms: what are the motivations, impacts, and consequences for mourners in terms of continuing bonds, expectations for future communications, and well-being in general?

Loss, grief, death, bereavement, and positive outcomes should be investigated, such as lower bereavement complications, positive identity changes, transformational grief, post-traumatic growth, resilience, and well-being. Most assume adverse outcomes for the bereaved, but death losses can facilitate growth.

The deceased's continued online presence through messages sent, applications that chat or advise, a hologram-type persona of the deceased, or similar such developments where the deceased "responds," may impact the grief and bereavement experience and adaptation after loss on a mourner. Such impacts and their implications for healthy outcomes should be carefully considered and investigated.

The advent of the digital world has produced many research opportunities for grief, loss, and dying practice and rituals in a digital context. It is emerging as a new area of practice and holds

Recommendations for Further Research and Study

promise in practice, innovation, education, and research. Scholarship in terms of new methodologies and superfluity in research possibilities presents an exciting era for researchers. Participants are many and varied as all people deal with death, dying, grief, and loss at some point. The ubiquitous nature of technology enables researchers to collaborate with other researchers and specialists across the globe. Dissemination of research is quick and effortless in a digital world. The fields of social sciences, physical sciences, education, theology, technologies, and more can collaborate across multidisciplinary areas to produce innovation, networks of information, education, and research.

Merging technologies for practitioners in grief, loss, death, and dying is possible and increases opportunities. A website could offer resources for mourners and caring professionals. Such a website may offer the following kinds of resources: videos; music; images; information; email functionality; links to counseling sessions with the choice of multiple caring professionals; spiritual and religious content and relevant links; information and links to palliative care providers; information on estates and wills; links to legal practitioners; links to applications for memorializing a deceased loved one with its own digital images and applications; links for arranging funerals or memorials with choices of coffins and flowers; digital visitor's books for attendants of funerals or memorials; and links to social networking platforms such as Facebook, Instagram, and YouTube with live tutorials, webinars, summits, workshops, and discussions or interviews. All of these things could run on one platform, and further add-ons, tools, and resources are possible. In short, everything death, grief, loss, and dying-related would be available in a "one-stop digital shop." We recommend examining the efficacy, sustainability, and ethics of such platforms and applications and the possibility of overwhelming, confusing, or "cheapening" the experience for bereaved clients.

Grief, loss, and bereavement are regarded as a sensitive area of research, which extends to the digital context. The use of questionnaires, assessments, surveys, and interventions, with associated research on the bereaved, can potentially harm. Deliberation of ethical considerations and mitigating factors is necessary. Such issues include anonymity, privacy issues (public vs. private), undue psychological and emotional distress, timing (period after a loss event), language used in questionnaires or interviews, the experience of researchers in this area, recruiting online mourners, and the criteria for studying bereaved participants (traumatic vs. nontraumatic death, relational proximity to the deceased, mental health diagnosis, and more). Further study into each of these factors and the potential for harm on the bereaved is advised, especially in the context of online grief and bereavement expressions and experiences and their unique circumstances. Approval for any research must be gained from university or other professional ethics committees.

Exploring the emerging area of grief, loss, death, and bereavement in a digital context is relatively new. We must be sensitive to participants and their needs. We must be willing to innovate, experiment, and creatively problem-solve. All this requires ethical consideration, must be open to researchers from multiple and intersecting disciplines, and consider the rapid changes in the online and technological fields.

9

Competent Care of the Soul Online

The emerging phenomenon of online interactions by the bereaved with the online presence of their deceased loved one has recently come to the attention of researchers and academics. In this book, we have explored the available theoretical and literary responses from interconnected areas of specialty. We have identified core themes of traditional Caucasian Euro-American loss, grief, and death ritual practices. We have compared and contrasted them with the processes and practices emerging in a digital context. After being previously sequestrated to medicalized and professionalized private practice, death and bereavement have been reintroduced to the public sphere. New issues such as the management and ownership of online interactions, digital estates and legacies, netiquette, "digital ghosts" and their impact, online grief support groups and communities, online memorials and more have arisen from these new and transferred rituals and practices.

This book has evaluated existing grief, loss, death, and bereavement theories and models and has considered their applications in a digital context. Such theories and models include grief work and stage or phase models, continuing bonds, attachment theory, dual processing theory, constructivism and meaning-making, adaptive grieving styles, and more. It is time helping professionals were equipped to explore spiritual concepts such as technospirituality and its associated "afterlife" expressions appropriately within the context of bereavement and social media.

Online bereavement and digital memorialization can aid in healthy grief, ritual, and memory for many people. However, as we've shown, caring professionals play a role in inviting people into the healing, well-being, and relationships that can only happen in the body and embodied community. Avoiding forms of cybergnosticism happens as we make the most of new technologies for human flourishing and as we seek embodied, enfleshed faith and fellowship. James K. A. Smith says that Christian worship and devotion always point in the direction of embodiment: "Implicit in Christian worship is a vision not just for spiritual flourishing but also for human flourishing; this is not just practice for eternal bliss; it is training for temporal, embodied human community."[1]

POINTING PEOPLE TO JESUS CHRIST'S LOVE AND PRESENCE

New or emerging loss, grief, and death practices that address the bereaved's needs in the digital age have been constructed spontaneously by mourners and introduced by caring professionals and death practitioners, some with unexpected and sometimes unwelcome digital reminders of the dead. This book has made various proposals for how counseling, pastoral, and spiritual care practitioners can help bereaved individuals navigate grief, loss, and death practices. Caring professionals can consider unique mourner needs, develop informed practice and education, join professional associations and governing bodies, reinterpret mourner needs, and create digital technologies and innovations.

Counselors, pastors, and spiritual carers have unique opportunities to support mourners and the bereaved in the digital age.

---

1. Smith, *Desiring the Kingdom*, 174.

Matthew 1 reminds us that our healing role is magnified as we point people to Immanuel's love and presence.

Ann Voskamp writes, "So God throws open the door of this world—and enters as a baby. As the most vulnerable imaginable. Because he wants unimaginable intimacy with you. What religion ever had a god that wanted such intimacy with us that he came with such vulnerability to us? What God ever came so tender we could touch him? So fragile that we could break him? So vulnerable that his bare, beating heart could be hurt? Only the One who loves you to death."[2]

It's often tempting to believe that the good life is a life of comfort, prosperity, safety, and ease. But this is rarely the case. Many of us discover peace, faith, and hope during difficult times. Our world is a world full of suffering, loss, and pain. Jesus entered and loved this world. Wherever we find ourselves in life, no matter what our dreams, losses, difficulties, or passions, we hear these striking words: "Immanuel; God is with us." God entered our world as a vulnerable and fragile child. God entered fully into this world of abuse and suffering and pain and war and violence and conflict. Jesus came as one fully exposed, completely vulnerable, exceedingly fragile, and shockingly tender.

"Immanuel" is the hope of our discipleship—our God is with us. God's strength for our weakness, faith for our doubt, joy for our tears, love for our hatred, hope for our disillusionment, light for our darkness, comfort for our distress, and healing for our pain and loss. God is with us; what will we fear? God is with us, filling us with incomparable faith, hope, and love.

This is the call of discipleship; that we live into the presence of "Immanuel, God with us." This is the role of the Christian healer, the Christian caring professional, pointing people to the love and presence of "Immanuel, God with us." The truth that "God is with us" is transforming, offering the healing, hope, and fullness of life that only Jesus Christ provides. Since God's presence is with us, we choose to live in the freedom of that presence. God's life becomes our fullness of life, God's healing our healing, God's hope

---

2. Voskamp, *Greatest Gift*, 83.

our hope, and God's future our future. Immanuel offers this hope and healing to all those who suffer and grieve in this digital age, as ever before.

Bibliography

Acciavatti, Michelle. "Guest Post—More Than a Funeral Service: Mediating Grief During Covid-19." *The Institute for the Study of Birth, Breath and Death*, March 29, 2020. https://birthbreathanddeath.com/death/guest-post-more-than-a-funeral-service-mediatating-grief-during-covid-19/.
The Acts of John. In *The Apocryphal New Testament,* edited by Montague R. James. Oxford: Clarendon, 1924.
"Apocryphon of John. (Ii, I)." In *The Nag Hammadi Library in English*, edited by James M. Robinson, 104–23. San Francisco: HarperOne, 1990.
Arai, Tosh, and S. Wesley Ariarajah. *Spirituality in Interfaith Dialogue.* Geneva: WCC, 1989.
Arntfield, Michael. "Ememoriam: Digital Necrologies, Virtual Remembrance, and the Question of Permanence." In *Digital Death: Mortality and Beyond in the Online Age*, edited by Christopher M. Moreman and A. David Lewis, 89–110. Westport, CT: Praeger, 2014.
BBC. "Facebook Is a Growing and Unstoppable Digital Graveyard." BBC, 2016. https://www.bbc.com/future/article/20160313-the-unstoppable-rise-of-the-facebook-dead.
Bell, Catherine M. *Ritual Theory, Ritual Practice.* New York: Oxford University Press, 1992.
Bell, Genevieve. "No More SMS from Jesus: Ubicomp, Religion and Techno-Spiritual Practices." In *Ubicomp 2006: Ubiquitous Computing*, edited by Paul Dourish and Adrian Friday, 141–58. Lecture Notes in Computer Science. Berlin: Springer, 2006.
Bell, Jo, et al. "'We Do It to Keep Him Alive': Bereaved Individuals' Experiences of Online Suicide Memorials and Continuing Bonds." *Mortality* 20, no. 4 (2015) 375–89.
Bennett, Jeffrey, and Jenny Huberman. "From Monuments to Megapixels: Death, Memory, and Symbolic Immortality in the Contemporary United States." *Anthropological Theory* 15, no. 3 (2015) 338–57.
Bianchi, Ugo, ed. *The Origins of Gnosticism: The Colloquium of Messina, 13–18 April.* Leiden: Brill, 1967.

Bibliography

Bogatin, Lisa, and Larry Lynn. "Aftertalk." In *Techniques of Grief Therapy*, edited by Robert A. Neimeyer, 232–35. Milton Park, Abingdon: Routledge, 2016.

Bourdeloie, Hélène. "Digital Lives of the Deceased: The Post-Mortem Data Uses." In *TEM 2015: Proceedings of the Technology and Emerging Media Track—Annual Conference*, edited by P. Dias da Silva and A. Alves, 2–12. Ottawa: Technology and Emerging Media, 2015.

Bowlby, John. *Loss: Sadness and Depression*. New York: Random House, 1998.

Breen, Lauren J., and Moira O'Connor. "The Fundamental Paradox in the Grief Literature: A Critical Reflection." *OMEGA—Journal of Death and Dying* 55, no. 3 (2007) 199–218.

Briggs, Pam, and Lisa Thomas. "The Social Value of Digital Ghosts." In *Digital Death: Mortality and Beyond in the Online Age*, edited by C. Moreman and A. D. Lewis, 125–42. Westport, CT: Praeger, 2014.

Brubaker, Jed R., and Gillian R. Hayes. "'We Will Never Forget You [Online]': An Empirical Investigation of Post-Mortem Myspace Comments." CSCW '11: Proceedings of the ACM 2011 conference on Computer Supported Cooperative Work, Hangzhou, China, ACM Digital Library, 2011.

Brubaker, Jed R., et al. "Beyond the Grave: Facebook as a Site for the Expansion of Death and Mourning." *The Information Society* 29, no. 3 (2013) 152–63.

Brubaker, Jed R., and Janet Vertesi. "Death and the Social Network." End of Life: ACM Conference on Human Factors in Computing Systems (CHI 2010), Atlanta, CHI, 2010.

Buckley, Jorunn Jacobsen. "Libertines or Not: Fruit, Bread, Semen and Other Body Fluids in Gnosticism." *Journal-of-Early-Christian-Studies* 2, no. 1 (1994) 15–31.

Burke, Laurie A., and Robert Neimeyer. "Spiritual Distress in Bereavement: Evolution of a Research Program." *Religions* 5, no. 4 (2014) 1087–1115.

Burke, Laurie A., et al. "Faith, Love, and Loss: When Belief and Bereavement Become Complicated." In *The Psychology of Love*, edited by Michelle Antoinette Paludi, 89–108. Westport, CT: Praeger, 2012.

Castro, Lusi A., and Victor M. Gonzales. "Afterlife Presence on Facebook: A Preliminary Examination of Wall Posts on the Deceased's Profiles." Conielecomp 2012: 22nd International Conference on Electrical Communications and Computers, Cholula, Puebla, February 2012.

Clines, David J. A. *Job 1–20*. Word Biblical Commentary, vol. 17. Nashville, TN: Thomas Nelson, 1989.

"Comparison between Web 2.0 and Web 3.0 Standards." K2B Solutions, 2014. https://www.k2bindia.com/comparison-between-web-2-0-and-web-3-0-standards/.

Conversation, Funeral Practitioners COVID 19. Facebook, March 23, 2020.

Dawson, Lorne L. "Religion and the Quest for Virtual Community." In *Religion Online: Finding Faith on the Internet*, edited by Lorne L. Dawson and Douglas E. Cowan, 75–92. Milton Park, Abingdon: Routledge, 2004.

Bibliography

Dermody, Erin. "Dark Tourism." In *Handbook of Sociology of Death, Grief, and Bereavement*, edited by Neil Thompson and Gerry R. Cox, 194–207. Milton Park, Abingdon: Routledge, 2017.

Di Lella, Alexander. "An Existential Interpretation of Job." *Biblical Theology* 15, no. 2 (1985) 49–55.

Doka, Kenneth J. "What's New in Grief? Current Trends in Grief Theory and Research." *Psychology Today*, February 11, 2016. https://www.psychologytoday.com/au/blog/good-mourning/201602/whats-new-in-grief.

Doka, Kenneth J., and Terry L. Martin. *Grieving Beyond Gender: Understanding the Ways Men and Women Mourn*. Milton Park, Abingdon: Routledge, 2011.

Doughty, Elizabeth A., and Wendy J. Hoskins. "Death Education: An Internationally Relevant Approach to Grief Counseling." *Journal for International Counselor Education* 3 (2011) 25–38. https://digitalscholarship.unlv.edu/cgi/viewcontent.cgi?article=1020&context=jice.

Doughty, Elizabeth A., et al. "Current Trends in Grief Counseling." *American Counseling Association VISTAS Online* 94 (2011) 1–10. https://counselingoutfitters.com/vistas/vistas11/Article_94.pdf.

Drenth, Cornelia, et al. "A Complicated Grief Intervention Programme (CGIP) for Social Workers." *Southern African Journal of Social Work and Social Development* 26, no. 3 (2017) 309–30.

Ebert, Heidi. "Profiles of the Dead: Mourning and Memorial on Facebook." In *Digital Death: Mortality and Beyond in the Online Age*, edited by Christopher M. Moreman and A. David Lewis, 23–42. Westport, CT: Praeger, 2014.

Edwards, Mark J. "Neglected Texts in the Study of Gnosticism." *Journal of Theological Studies* 41, no. 1 (1990) 26–49.

Filoramo, Giovanni. *A History of Gnosticism*. Oxford: Basil Blackwell, 1990.

Fiorini, Leticia Glocer, et al. *On Freud's Mourning and Melancholia*. Milton Park, Abingdon: Routledge, 2018.

Fowler, Hayley. "'Drive-in Funeral Theater' Helps Families Mourn During Coronavirus Shutdown in Texas Read." *The News Tribune* (2020). https://www.thenewstribune.com/news/business/article242041066.html.

Freud, Sigmund. "Mourning and Melancholia." In *The Standard Edition of the Complete Psychological Works of Sigmund Freud*, edited by James Strachey, 243–58. London: Hogarth, 1957.

Frost, Michael. "Christians, Engaged and Incarnate." *Christianity Today: Pastors* (2014). https://www.christianitytoday.com/pastors/2014/may-online-only/moving-from-excarnation-to-incarnation.html.

———. *Incarnate: The Body of Christ in an Age of Disengagement*. Downers Grove, IL: InterVarsity, 2014.

Fuller, Reginald H., and Pheme Perkins. *Who Is This Christ?: Gospel Christology and Contemporary Faith*. Philadelphia, PA: Fortress, 1983.

Bibliography

Gamino, Louis. "Ethical Considerations When Conducting Grief Counseling and Pastoral and Spiritual Care Online." In *Dying, Death, and Grief in an Online Universe*, edited by Carla J. Sofka, Illene Noppe Cupit, and Kathleen R. Gilbert, 217–34. New York: Springer, 2012.

Gercama, Ingrid, and Theresa Jones. "Alternative Mourning Rituals Offer Comfort and Closure During an Outbreak." *NPR* (2020). https://www.npr.org/sections/goatsandsoda/2020/04/02/793951420/new-mourning-rituals-offer-comfort-and-closure-during-an-outbreak.

Giaxoglou, Korina, et al. "Networked Emotions: Interdisciplinary Perspectives on Sharing Loss Online." *Journal of Broadcasting and Electronic Media* 61, no. 1 (March 7, 2017) 1–10.

Gilbert, Kathleen R. "Death, Grief and Virtual Connections: The Role of Social Media for Social Support and Memorialization." In *Handbook of the Sociology of Death, Grief, and Bereavement*, edited by Neil Thompson and Gerry R. Cox, 291–305. Milton Park, Abingdon: Routledge, 2017.

Gilbert, Kathleen R., and Michael Massimi. "From Digital Divide to Digital Immortality: Thanatechnology at the Turn of the 21st Century." In *Dying, Death, and Grief in an Online Universe*, edited by Carla J. Sofka, Illene Noppe Cupit, and Kathleen R. Gilbert, 16–30. New York: Springer, 2012.

Gilhus, Ingvild Sælid. "Gnosticism: A Study in Liminal Symbolism." *Numen* 31, no. 1 (1984) 106–28.

Granek, Leeat. "Is Grief a Disease? The Medicalization of Grief by the Psy-Disciplines in the Twenty-First Century." In *Handbook of the Sociology of Death, Grief, and Bereavement*, edited by Neil Thompson and Gerry R. Cox, 264–77. Milton Park, Abingdon: Routledge, 2017.

Grant, Robert M. "Gnostic Spirituality." In *Christian Spirituality: Origins to the Twelfth Century*, edited by Bernard McGinn, John Meyendorff, and Jean Leclerc, 44–60. New York: Crossroad, 1985.

Green, Henry A. *The Economic and Social Origins of Gnosticism*. Atlanta: Scholars, 1985.

Group, Parent Loss Grief Support. Facebook, January 12, 2017.

Hagman, George. *New Models of Bereavement Theory and Treatment: New Mourning*. Milton Park, Abingdon: Routledge, 2016.

Hamilton, Malcolm B. *The Sociology of Religion: Theoretical and Comparative Perspectives*. 2d ed. Milton Park, Abingdon: Routledge, 1995.

Hartley, John E. *The Book of Job*. The New International Commentary on the Old Testament. Grand Rapids: Eerdmans, 1988.

Hedrick, Charles W., and Robert Hodgson, eds. *Nag Hammadi, Gnosticism, and Early Christianity: Fourteen Leading Scholars Discuss the Current Issues in Gnostic Studies*. Peabody, MA: Hendrickson, 1986.

Hieftje, Kimberly. "The Role of Social Networking Sites in Memorialization of College Students." In *Dying, Death, and Grief in an Online Universe*, edited by Carla J. Softka, Illene Noppe Cupit, and Kathleen R. Gilbert, 31–46. New York: Springer, 2012.

Bibliography

Hollenback, Kacy L. "Ritual and Religion." In *Behavioral Archaeology: Principles and Practice*, edited by Michael B. Schiffer, 156–63. Milton Park, Abingdon: Routledge, 2010.

Hoy, William G. *Do Funerals Matter? The Purposes and Practices of Death Rituals in Global Perspective*. Milton Park, Abingdon: Routledge, 2013.

Hultgren, Arland J., and Steven A. Haggmark, eds. *The Early Christian Heretics: Readings from Their Opponents*. Minneapolis: Fortress, 1996.

Hutchings, Tim. "Death, Emotion and Digital Media." In *Emotions and Religious Dynamics*, edited by Douglas J. Davies and Nathaniel A. Warne, 191–212. Oxon: Routledge, 2016.

———. "Wiring Death: Dying, Grieving and Remembering on the Internet." In *Emotion, Identity and Death: Mortality across Disciplines*, edited by Douglas J. Davies and Chang-Won Park, 43–58. Burlington, VA: Ashgate, 2012.

Irenaeus. "Against Heresies 1.7.5." In *The Religious Context of Early Christianity: A Guide to Graeco-Roman Religions*, edited by Hans Jonas, 469. Minneapolis: Fortress, 2003.

James, John, and Russell Friedman. *The Grief Recovery Handbook: The Action Program for Moving Beyond Death, Divorce, and Other Losses Including Health, Career, and Faith*. New York: Harper Collins, 2009.

James, Montague Rhodes, ed. *The Apocryphal New Testament*. Oxford: Clarendon, 1924.

Jonas, Hans. "Gnosis Und Spatantiker Geist, 1:259, in Waldstein, Michael, 2000, 'Hans Jonas' Construct "Gnosticism": Analysis and Critique.'" *Journal of Early Christian Studies* 8, no. 3 (January 2000) 341–72.

———. *The Gnostic Religion: The Message of the Alien God and the Beginnings of Christianity*. Milton Park, Abingdon: Routledge, 1992.

———. *The Religious Context of Early Christianity: A Guide to Graeco-Roman Religions*. Minneapolis: Fortress, 2003.

———. "Return to the Divine Origin: The Gnostic Transformation." In *The Religious Context of Early Christianity: A Guide to Graeco-Roman Religions*, edited by Hans Jonas, 429–98. Minneapolis: Fortress, 2003.

Jones, B. D. *Dwell: Life with God for the World*. Downers Grove, IL: InterVarsity, 2014.

Jones, Jasenka. "Towards an Understanding of Death in Ireland in the Digital Age." MA thesis, University College, 2014.

Klass, Dennis, and Tony Walter. "Processes of Grieving: How Bonds Are Continued." In *Handbook of Bereavement Research: Consequences, Coping, and Care*, edited by Margaret S. Stroebe, Robert O. Hansson, Wolfgang Stroebe, and Henk Schut, 431–48. Washington, DC: American Psychological Association, 2001.

Kübler-Ross, Elisabeth. *On Death and Dying*. New York: Scribner, 1969.

Kushner, Harold S. *When Bad Things Happen to Good People*. New York: Anchor, 2004.

———. "Why Do the Righteous Suffer? Notes toward a Theology of Tragedy." *Judaism* 28, no. 3 (Summer 1979) 316–23.

Lash, Nicholas. *Believing Three Ways in One God: A Reading of the Apostles' Creed*. Notre Dame, IN: University of Notre Dame Press, 1993.

Lewis, C. S. *A Grief Observed*. San Francisco: HarperSanFrancisco, 2001.

———. *The Problem of Pain*. Macmillan Paperbacks ed. New York: Macmillan, 1962.

Logan, Alastair. "At-Onement: The Nature and Challenge of Gnostic Soteriology." *Scottish Journal of Theology* 50, no. 4 (1997) 481–98.

———. *Gnostic Truth and Christian Heresy: A Study in the History of Gnosticism*. Edinburgh: T. & T. Clark, 1997.

———. "Truth in a Heresy? Gnosticism Source." *Expository Times* 112, no. 6 (2001) 187–91.

Logan, Alastair, and Alexander J. M. Wedderburn, eds. *The New Testament and Gnosis: Essays in Honor of Robert McL. Wilson*. Edinburgh: T. & T. Clark, 1983.

Lynn, Cendra, and Antje Rath. "Griefnet: Creating and Maintaining an Internet Bereavement Community." In *Dying, Death, and Grief in an Online Universe*, edited by Carla J. Sofka, Illene Noppe Cupit, and Kathleen R. Gilbert, 217–34. New York: Springer, 2012.

McEwen, Rhonda N., and Kathleen Scheaffer. "Virtual Mourning and Memory Construction on Facebook: Here Are the Terms of Use." *Proceedings of The American Society for Information Science and Technology* 50, no. 1 (2013) 1–10.

Milman, Evgenia, et al. "Prolonged Grief Symptomatology Following Violent Loss: The Mediating Role of Meaning." *European Journal of Psychotraumatology* 8, no. 6 (2018) 69–78.

Naik, Umesha, and D. Shivalingaiah. "Comparative Study of Web 1.0, Web 2.0 and Web 3.0." 6th International CALIBER—2008, INFLIBNET Centre, Ahmedabad, Information and Library Network (INFLIBNET) Centre, 2008.

Nansen, Bjorn, et al. "The Restless Dead in Digital Cemetery." In *Digital Death: Mortality and Beyond in the Online Age*, edited by Christopher M. Moreman and A. David Lewis, 111–24. Westport, CT: Praeger, 2012.

Niemeyer, Robert A., and Jason M. Holland. "Bereavement in Later Life: Theory, Assessment and Intervention." In *APA Handbook of Clinical Geropsychology*, edited by Benjamin T. Mast and Peter A. Lichtenberg, 2–53. Washington, DC: American Psychological Association, 2015.

Neimeyer, Robert A., et al. "Continuing Bonds and Reconstructing Meaning: Mitigating Complications in Bereavement." *Death Studies* 30, no. 8 (2006) 715–38.

Network, Professionals Grief and Loss. Facebook, April 29, 2018.

Newman, Elizabeth. "Theology and Science without Dualism." *Cross Currents* 48, no. 1 (1998) 34–48.

Bibliography

Novak, Kori D. "An Examination of Grief and Bereavement Theories in Human Service Practice." PhD diss., South University, 2010. https://www.academia.edu/15334073/An_Examination_of_Grief_and_Bereavement_Theories_in_Human_Service_Practice.

"Number of Monthly Active Facebook Users Worldwide as of 4th Quarter 2020." Statista, 2020. https://www.statista.com/statistics/264810/number-of-monthly-active-facebook-users-worldwide/.

Page, Funeral Professionals Corona Discussion. Facebook, March 17, 2020.

Pagels, Elaine H. *The Gnostic Gospels*. London: Weidenfeld and Nicolson, 1980.

———. *The Gnostic Paul: Gnostic Exegesis of the Pauline Letters*. Philadelphia: Trinity, 1975.

———. *The Johannine Gospel in Gnostic Exegesis*. Nashville, TN: Abingdon, 1973.

"Paraphrase of Shem." In *The Nag Hammadi Library in English*, edited by James M. Robinson, 339–61. San Francisco: HarperOne, 1990.

Pearson, Birger A. "Early Christianity and Gnosticism in the History of Religions." *Studia Theologica* 55, no. 1 (2001) 81–106.

———. "Eusebius and Gnosticism." In *Eusebius, Christianity, and Judaism*, edited by Harold W. Attridge and Gohei Hata, 291–310. Detroit: Wayne State University Press, 1992.

———. "Gnosticism as Platonism: With Special Reference to Marsanes (Nhc 10,1)." *Harvard Theological Review* 77, no. 1 (1984) 55–72.

Perkins, John M. *Dream with Me: Race, Love, and the Struggle We Must Win*. Grand Rapids: Baker, 2017.

Perkins, Pheme. "Creation of the Body in Gnosticism." In *Religious Reflections on the Human Body*, edited by Jane Marie Law, 21–35. Bloomington, IN: Indiana University Press, 1995.

———. *The Gnostic Dialogue: The Early Church and the Crisis of Gnosticism*. New York: Paulist, 1980.

———. *Gnosticism and the New Testament*. Minneapolis: Fortress, 1993.

Quispel, Gilles. "The Original Doctrine of Valentinus the Gnostic." *Vigiliae-Christianae* 50, no. 4 (1996) 327–52.

Renwick, Alexander Macdonald. "Gnosticism." In *The International Standard Bible Encyclopedia*, edited by Geoffrey W. Bromiley, 484–86. Grand Rapids: Eerdmans, 1982.

Robinson, James M., ed. *The Nag Hammadi Library in English*. San Francisco, CA: HarperSanFrancisco, 1990.

Rudolph, Kurt. *Gnosis: The Nature and History of an Ancient Religion*. Edinburgh: T. & T. Clark, 1983.

———. "'Gnosis' and 'Gnosticism': The Problems of Their Definition and Their Relation to the Writings of the New Testament." In *The New Testament and Gnosis*, edited by Alastair Logan and Alexander J. M. Wedderburn, 34–52. Edinburgh: T. & T. Clark, 1983.

Bibliography

Sanderson, Jimmy, and Pauline Hope Cheong. "Tweeting Prayers and Communicating Grief over Michael Jackson Online." *Bulletin of Science, Technology and Society* 30, no. 5 (2010) 328–40.

Shelley, Mary. *Frankenstein: The Modern Prometheus*. Barnes & Noble Classics. New York: Fine Creative Media, 2004.

Smith, James K. A. *Desiring the Kingdom: Worship, Worldview, and Cultural Formation*. Volume 1 of Cultural Liturgies. Grand Rapids: Baker Academic, 2009.

Sofka, Carla J. "The Net Generation: The Special Case of Youth." In *Dying, Death, and Grief in an Online Universe*, edited by Carla J. Sofka, Illene Noppe Cupit, and Kathleen R. Gilbert, 47–60. New York: Springer, 2012.

Sofka, Carla J., et al. "Thanatechnology as a Conduit for Living, Dying, and Grieving in Contemporary Society." In *Dying, Death, and Grief in an Online Universe*, edited by Carla J. Sofka, Illene Noppe Cupit, and Kathleen R. Gilbert, 3–15. New York: Springer, 2012.

Staley, Erinn. "Messaging the Dead: Social Network Sites and Theologies of Afterlife." In *Digital Death: Mortality and Beyond in the Online Age*, edited by Christopher M. Moreman and A. David Lewis, 9–22. Westport, CT: Praeger, 2014.

Stewart, Pamela J., and Andrew Stratham. *Ritual: Key Concepts in Religion*. London: Bloomsbury, 2014.

Stillman, Ari. "Virtual Graveyard: Facebook, Death, and Existentialist Critique." In *Digital Death: Mortality and Beyond in the Online Age*, edited by Christopher M. Moreman and A. David Lewis, 43–68. Westport, CT: Praeger, 2014.

Strobel, Kyle. *Metamorpha: Jesus as a Way of Life*. Grand Rapids: Baker, 2007.

Stroebe, Margaret S., et al., eds. *Handbook of Bereavement Research: Consequences, Coping, and Care*. Washington, DC: American Psychological Association, 2001.

Stroebe, Margaret, and Henk Schut. "The Dual Process Model of Coping with Bereavement: Rationale and Description." *Death Studies* 23, no. 3 (1999) 197–224.

Stroebe, Margaret, et al. "Attachment in Coping with Bereavement: A Theoretical Integration." *Review of General Psychology* 9, no. 1 (2005) 48–66.

Stroebe, Margaret, et al. "Continuing Bonds in Adaptation to Bereavement: Toward Theoretical Integration." *Clinical Psychology Review* 30, no. 2 (2010) 259–68.

Tertullian. "Prescription against Heretics. 41." In *The Apocryphal New Testament*, edited by Montague Rhodes James, 228–66. Oxford: Clarendon, 1924.

Thompson, Neil. "The Role of Religion and Spirituality in Grieving." In *Handbook of the Sociology of Death, Grief, and Bereavement*, edited by Neil Thompson and Gerry R. Cox, 337–50. Milton Park, Abingdon: Routledge, 2017.

Tilley, Terrence W. "God and the Silencing of Job." *Modern Theology* 5, no. 3 (April 1989) 257–70.

Bibliography

"Treatise on the Resurrection. 47:17–19." In *The Nag Hammadi Library in English*, edited by James M. Robinson, 52. San Francisco: HarperOne, 1990.

Van Ryn, Luke, et al. "Researching Death Online." In *The Routledge Companion to Digital Ethnography*, edited by Larissa Hjorth, Heather Horst, Anne Galloway, and Genevieve Bell, 112–20. Milton Park, Abingdon: Routledge, 2017.

Voskamp, Ann. *The Greatest Gift: Unwrapping the Full Love Story of Christmas*. Carol Stream, IL: Tyndale, 2013.

Wagner, Birgit, and Andreas Maercker. "Internet-Based Writing." In *Techniques of Grief Therapy*, edited by Robert A. Neimeyer, 201–4. Milton Park, Abingdon: Routledge, 2016.

Walter, Tony. "New Mourners, Old Mourners: Online Memorial Culture as a Chapter in the History of Mourning." *New Review of Hypermedia and Multimedia* 21, no. 1–2 (2015) 10–24.

———. "Why Different Countries Manage Death Differently: A Comparative Analysis of Modern Urban Societies." *The British Journal of Sociology* 63, no. 1 (2012) 123–45.

Walter, Tony, et al. "Does the Internet Change How We Die and Mourn? Overview and Analysis." *OMEGA—Journal of Death and Dying* 64, no. 4 (2012) 275–302.

"What Is a Social Networking Site (SNS)?" Janalta, 2017. https://www.techopedia.com/definition/4956/social-networking-site-SNS.

"What Is Web 2.0?" ZNet Technologies, May 13, 2016. https://www.znetlive.com/blog/web-2-0/.

Williams, Michael Allen. "Anticosmic World-Rejection? Or Sociocultural Accommodation?" In *Rethinking "Gnosticism": An Argument for Dismantling a Dubious Category*, edited by Michael Allen Williams, 96–115. Princeton, NJ: Princeton University Press, 1996.

———. *Rethinking "Gnosticism": An Argument for Dismantling a Dubious Category*. Princeton, NJ: Princeton University Press, 1996.

Wilson, Robert McLachlan. "Slippery Words, 2: Gnosis, Gnostic, Gnosticism." *Expository Times* 89, no. 10 (1978) 296–301.

Worden, J. William. *Grief Counseling and Grief Therapy: A Handbook for the Mental Health Practitioner*. 5th ed. New York: Springer, 2018.

About the Authors

GRAHAM JOSEPH HILL

Graham Joseph Hill lives in Sydney, Australia. He is Principal of Stirling Theological College (University of Divinity) and Associate Professor of Global Christianity. Graham's author website is www.grahamjosephhill.com. Graham has planted and pastored churches and been in theological education for over twenty years. He is the author or editor of eleven books, including *Holding Up Half the Sky*; *Hide This in Your Heart* (co-authored with Michael Frost); *Global Church*; *Healing Our Broken Humanity* (co-authored with Grace Ji-Sun Kim); and *Salt, Light, and a City* (two volumes). Graham also directs TheGlobalChurchProject.com.

DESIREE GELDENHUYS

Desiree Geldenhuys lives on the Gold Coast, Australia. Desiree is Tutor in Counseling at Stirling Theological College (University of Divinity). She trained as an economist and worked in financial markets for almost two decades but always had a passion for counseling, psychotherapy, and helping people. Desiree is a Clinical Counsellor, Clinical Member of the College of Supervisors with the Australian Counseling Association (ACA), and a member of the College of Grief and Loss Counsellors (Australia). Desiree runs a private counseling, family therapy, and supervision practice. She has done extensive research in the areas of bereavement, grief, and loss. Desiree has worked as a chaplain, is a counsellor in both primary and secondary school, a charity director, and a Lifeline volunteer (a crisis support service).

www.ingramcontent.com/pod-product-compliance
Lightning Source LLC
Chambersburg PA
CBHW031503160426
43195CB00010BB/1092